Praise for *Parenting with Heart*

"*Parenting with Heart* is a radical and compelling book for parents and grandparents, who know in their heart parenting is not easy. It is foolish to believe something as important as parenting can be legislated into a few steps or principles. James and Dodd offer a map to guide your engagement with your children and the wisdom to do so humbly, even in the face of inevitable struggles. Parenting changes us all, but often it turns us more toward guilt or worry. This brilliant resource will give you a path for joy and rich relationships with your children. You (and your children) will not be the same after reading this book."

Dan B. Allender, PhD, professor of counseling psychology
and founding president of The Seattle School of Theology
and Psychology; author of *Healing the Wounded Heart*
and *How Children Raise Parents*

"Stephen James and Chip Dodd have invited you into their counseling offices in this book. They have created a safe space for you to grow as a parent—to learn, to laugh, to be honest about your vulnerability and imperfection, and to discover. You will finish this book with more hope, more understanding, and more grace—for both your child and yourself."

Sissy Goff, MEd, LPC-MHSP, director of child and
adolescent counseling, Daystar Counseling Ministries;
speaker; and author of numerous books,
including *Are My Kids on Track?*

"Every beleaguered parent who reads this book is going to let out a massive sigh of relief. Finally, a book that is not telling them what to do and how they are not measuring up. Stephen James and Chip Dodd do a masterful job of defining God's high calling in the life of a parent without adding to their collective sense of regret and guilt for not being 'perfect.' I had to laugh out loud when I read the subheading, 'Clumsy is as good as it gets'! And all the parents said, 'Amen!'"

Jimmy Myers, PhD, LPC-S, coauthor of *Fearless Parenting: How to Raise Faithful Kids in a Secular Culture*

"I trust Chip Dodd and Stephen James. I trust and value their work as counselors and teachers. More importantly, I trust them as people and as fathers themselves. These wise men are inviting us into a more sustainable way to parent the kids we love, whatever ages they may be. Chip and Stephen are showing us how to be clumsy and courageous at the same time. I will recommend this book to countless parents, and I'll be revisiting this rich content as a dad myself."

David Thomas, LMSW, director of family counseling, Daystar Counseling Ministries; coauthor of eight books, including *Intentional Parenting*

"As Stephen James and Chip Dodd so effectively articulate, parenting with heart is infinitely more wonderful—and more challenging!—than trying to control our kids' behavior and future. While we may think having happy, successful children is the highest goal, that's a poor substitute for raising kids who can love and learn from life on life's terms. Stephen and Chip share vulnerably from their own parenting journeys, guiding those of us who long to embrace the adventure and freedom of being full-hearted parents. In reading this book, you will grow and be transformed, which means your children will grow and be transformed too. Don't settle for endless striving to be a 'perfect' parent. Follow Stephen and Chip and be a gloriously clumsy, fabulously good-enough parent instead."

Dr. Jeramy and Jerusha Clark, authors of several books, including the award-winning *Your Teenager Is Not Crazy: Understanding Your Teen's Brain Can Make You a Better Parent*

HOPE
IN THE AGE OF
ADDICTION

HOPE

IN THE AGE OF

ADDICTION

HOW TO FIND FREEDOM AND RESTORE
—— YOUR RELATIONSHIPS ——

CHIP DODD AND
STEPHEN JAMES

Revell

a division of Baker Publishing Group
Grand Rapids, Michigan

Published by Revell
a division of Baker Publishing Group
PO Box 6287, Grand Rapids, MI 49516-6287
www.revellbooks.com

Printed in the United States of America

Library of Congress Cataloging-in-Publication Data
Names: Dodd, Chip, author. | James, Stephen, 1973– author.
Title: Hope in the age of addiction : how to find freedom and restore your relationships / Chip Dodd and Stephen James.
Description: Grand Rapids, Michigan : Revell, a division of Baker Publishing Group, 2020.
Identifiers: LCCN 2020004894 | ISBN 9780800729400 (paperback)
Subjects: LCSH: Addicts—Religious life. | Addicts—Pastoral counseling of. | Substance abuse—Religious aspects—Christianity. | Compulsive behavior—Religious aspects—Christianity.
Classification: LCC BV4596.A24 D64 2020 | DDC 248.8/629—dc23
LC record available at https://lccn.loc.gov/2020004894

20   21   22   23   24   25   26   7   6   5   4   3   2   1

To all those who live in freedom from addiction and are part of the solution, and to all those who are still searching for freedom and who we pray will find recovery of who they are created to be.

I do not understand what I do. For what I want to do I do not do, but what I hate I do. . . . As it is, it is no longer I myself who do it, but it is sin living in me. . . . For I have the desire to do what is good, but I cannot carry it out. For I do not do the good I want to do, but the evil I do not want to do—this I keep on doing.

Paul (Rom. 7:15, 17–19)

CONTENTS

ACKNOWLEDGMENTS

We thank the GOD who meets us in our neediness and through his presence and power returns people to full life.

Any attempt to address the topic of addiction and recovery in a meaningful and helpful way requires that we go behind the front doors of peoples' lives. Addiction is personal. We want to thank the women and men who have shared their stories of recovery that make up so much of this book. Their courage and vulnerability is admirable.

We also want to recognize and thank the professionals who work in the field of addiction with integrity and character. Whether as therapists, pastors, sponsors, physicians, or others, these people do the daily work of offering their experience, strength, and hope to those who need it the most.

We also express our gratitude to those mentors and collaborators who have shared with us their knowledge and care that allow and enable us to create the summative work. We have been assisted personally and professionally all along our careers. Some of their influence clearly has found its way into this work. For that we are grateful.

Thank you to the team at Revell for having the courage to publish a work that could be easily neglected because it's both ubiquitous and difficult to address. Specifically, Vicki Crumpton, our acquisitions editor, who helped us clarify and wrangle the early manuscripts into being more accessible to readers. Also thank you to Gisèle Mix, our project editor, who kept us on track and further polished the manuscript, and Melinda Timmer, who added valuable editorial feedback that enhanced the clarity and readability. Thanks also to the marketing and publicity team for getting this book out there. Our world is in desperate need of direction and hope to overcome the snares of addiction.

Thank you to our agent, Greg Daniel, for bringing calm to the storm of the writing process. It's not always easy working with us.

Above all, we want to thank our families for being the most honest and caring teachers we will ever have.

AUTHORS' NOTE

Between the chapters in this book are stories of recovery told by people in their own words.

These stories of life, addiction, and recovery are true. They are NOT clinical vignettes. They are the real words of extraordinary people who through hope, courage, honesty, willingness, community, prayer, grief, and joy have found lives free of the bondage and torture of addiction.

The brave and generous women and men who wrote them took the risk of vulnerability in the hope that their pain, struggle, and freedom from addiction could help to encourage others in their own healing and recovery.

Since many of these stories contain pieces of information about people other than the storytellers, after much consideration it was decided that specific identifying information, such as names and locations, would be altered. These minor fact changes in no way make these stories less truthful or less encouraging.

Thank you for reading this book and their stories. We hope they bless and encourage you.

Keep Heart,
Chip and Stephen

A LETTER TO THOSE
WHO ARE IN ADDICTION

Dear Friend,

There is hope. Whether you are addicted to alcohol, pills, people, technology, sex, or work, there is hope.

The truth is that underneath your denial and wishful thinking, you hear the "whispers in the night" that say you have a problem. You want to call it stress. You want to call it depression, or burnout, or being controlled, or having to perform, or coping with trauma. While those things are real, and do not need to be minimized, they do not accurately name the problem.

No amount of rearranging your circumstances, no amount of better thinking, stronger discipline, or moral promises and actions will change your problem. Only admitting what you hear in the whispers in the night will help you.

The whispers say, "You have a problem." Something is quietly destroying your life. You have become powerless over something that you can't stop doing, even though the negative consequences are beginning to pile up.

You will have a hard time accepting this, but addiction is not your fault. You have addiction; you are not addiction. No one plans to be stuck in secret despair, misery, or pretending. No one desires to have to keep moving to avoid the anxiety of being with one's self. Addiction is something that begins as a solution to emotional, psychological, spiritual, or physical discomfort and becomes a sickness. It starts as a friend and then becomes the master. No one sets out to become enslaved, but enslaved you become. The thing you cannot stop doing to comfort yourself, feel safe, and feel connected is your problem.

You have a sickness, not a sin. We cannot stress enough that addiction is a sickness, not a "badness." Yes, you sin all the more because of how you cling to the thing that enslaves you. But the "sin" doesn't stop until the sickness is in remission. The person who is most harmed in addiction is the person who has the addiction. From that point of harm, everyone around you begins to suffer.

You are not crazy, but your thinking and your perspective are clouded and controlled by addiction. You didn't cause your addiction, but you are responsible for facing it and getting help. That healing starts by admitting that you are powerless over your addiction and that your life has become unmanageable because of it. Facing and feeling this reality takes work and the help of others who know addiction's power. You have to reach out to others who have the recovery you want and become willing to follow their ways. In the beginning, you may not like doing this and just simply comply. Eventually, as your denial fades, your emotional wounds will heal, your anxiety will subside, your depression will lift, and many of your relationships will be restored. You will begin to see clearly again through the eyes of your heart.

As you surrender to help, you will find that underneath the addiction you have a heart problem. You don't know what to do with or how to handle the feelings, needs, desire, longings, and hopes that were instilled in you at birth. Through the process of recovery, you will regain your birthright, and you will get to return to living in relationship with yourself, others, and God.

No matter how much or how little you have achieved in the world, no matter how admired you are or rejected you feel, God sees you and loves you. Whether you are a believer in God or not, God whispers hope to you. God loves you where you are and wants more for you than you have ever allowed yourself to have. Others in recovery await you with their hands, heads, and especially their hearts to show you the love you don't believe in.

We pray that you will reach out for the help that awaits you and the life you can have. We each have taken that risk to reach out for help, and it has made all the difference in our own lives and in the lives of those we most love. We have seen thousands of others do the same. It can be true for you as well.

In love,
Chip and Stephen

A LETTER TO THOSE WHO LOVE SOMEONE WHO IS IN ADDICTION

Dear Friend,

You are reading this book because you have hope. You are also reading this book because you are likely in pain. Someone you love deeply is suffering in addiction, and it is breaking your heart and impacting your life. You are not the problem. You are neither failing nor defective. God has not left you. You are not alone. There is help and hope available.

Addiction is a contagious sickness; it affects everyone who is in relationship with it. Addiction is what a person has. It is not who they are. Underneath the addiction is the person you once knew and hope to meet again.

We know firsthand the pain and heartache that addiction causes and the repercussions that can last decades—if not generations. Both of us were raised in families that were infected by addiction. Also, as counselors, we have worked in the devastation of addiction and the hope of redemption for over fifty years combined. We have witnessed addiction, like quicksand, slowly pull people, families, organizations, and even entire cultures into despair, apathy, and death.

I (Chip) remember the late-night prayers of my childhood as I lay in my bed trying to sleep but I couldn't because I was so scared. I remember the secret keeping, the pretending, and the denial of what was obvious to others. I remember the loss of my own self-worth and the toxic shame of believing that something was inherently wrong with me, that somehow I was responsible for the problems. I remember the need to maintain the status quo by saying and doing whatever needed to be said and done to keep the boat afloat.

Even as addiction continued to flood the hull of our family boat, we kept reconfiguring the deck chairs as a solution instead of seeing the real problem. I couldn't be good enough, smart enough, caring enough, tough enough, sensitive enough, thoughtful enough, pleasing enough, distracting enough, funny enough, or even in denial enough to change things.

You can't either. The problem of addiction is bigger than you are. Neither containing it nor denying it stops it. You are surviving in an environment that addiction controls.

Your solution is to get help for yourself. This is important. Reaching out for your own healing and recovery is the best thing you can do for the person who has the addiction.

As you begin your own recovery of heart, you may experience a sense of shame—as if you are somehow betraying your loved one. You aren't betraying them. You are, however, bravely rejecting the control addiction has over your life and those you love.

Your emotional, spiritual, psychological, and physical health and recovery are of primary significance. Your recovery brings light into the darkness and hope into discouragement. As you get help, heal, and grow, you will have a greater ability to help the one you love in addiction.

When you fly on an airplane, the instructions before takeoff tell you that in an emergency you are to "put the mask over your own face first before you attempt to assist anyone else." If you love someone in addiction, taking care of yourself first seems counterintuitive, but if you are in chaos or in denial, you can't help someone else.

Addiction has control through secrecy. Break the secrecy and let others into your life. Please take the risk of reaching out. Even if you are not sure that addiction is the problem, seek help from those people who know what addiction is and have knowledge and experience in recovery from addiction and recovery of heart. As you reach beyond surviving addiction and reach out to others who have found the freedom we talk about in this book, you will find people to encourage your hope, help you gain recovery of heart, and establish sanity amid the insanity of addiction.

Others will help you with their stories. You will be able to relate to them, and they will support your risks. They will encourage your steps to regain the truth of living. They will assist you in beginning to see things anew, in

21

some ways as if the scales have fallen from your eyes. Your recovery work will allow you to begin to thrive again.

You can find these people to help you in the therapeutic process of recovery, from the therapist who understands how to help in addiction to those in recovery you will meet through the many groups that exist for recovery. (Groups such as Al-Anon, Adult Children of Alcoholics, and Celebrate Recovery are in almost every town.)

Our prayer for you is that you will gain strength and courage, more than knowledge, from this book. We have been able to see firsthand thousands of people find freedom from addiction. We know the hard work of risking, of walking through the toxic shame and the fear of being rejected for having our own feelings and needs. We remember the depths of grieving losses, terror, wounds, and aloneness that addiction inflicts on those it touches. We also remember regaining the Self we each lost. We remember being able to live fully again in relationship with God and others—becoming trusting of love and being able to love openheartedly again. Going beyond survival and returning to thriving were worth every step and every tear.

We pray that you and your loved ones will find the healing and the freedom that are real and available. We are emotional and spiritual creatures, created to find full life in relationship with our own hearts, the hearts of others, and the heart of God. Others and the God who has always loved you and wants to show you more love will meet you in your reach for help.

Keep Heart,
Chip and Stephen

INTRODUCTION

You are loved.
You come from love, and your destiny is love.
You are free to create.
Your heart has been broken, and it will likely be again.
Your heart is resilient.

Life is tragic and painful.
Life is rough and not fair.
Life is beautiful and fleeting.
Life is meaningful and poetic.

God is.
God is who God is.
God is unfathomable.
God is powerful.
God is faithful.
God is love.

This list—about you, life, and God—is what this book is about.

So what does this list have to do with addiction? Read it again, more slowly this time. Notice what words, images, stories, ideas, and feelings come to you. Maybe even jot down some notes.

You are loved.

You come from love, and your destiny is love.

You are free to create.

Your heart has been broken, and it will likely be again.

Your heart is resilient.

Life is tragic and painful.

Life is rough and not fair.

Life is beautiful and fleeting.

Life is meaningful and poetic.

God is.

God is who God is.

God is unfathomable.

God is powerful.

God is faithful.

God is love.

This list is in no way exhaustive. Every person could add so much more, but whatever we could add would just help to make the point that life is full of tension, paradox, heartache, truth, beauty, and mystery—most of which we can never fully understand. To paraphrase the apostle Paul, we see through a smoky glass, seeing only slivers of the bigger picture (1 Cor. 13:12). But just because we can't fully understand doesn't mean we won't stop trying to reconcile the complexities and difficulties of life. It's almost like we are compelled to or made to, while at the same time we have to struggle to accept our limitations.

Hearts Made to Live Fully and Free

All of us have made many attempts to make life work the way we want it to work. We try with everything in us to reconcile, express, and understand the various aspects of life. Every philosophy, religion, theological system, social code, scientific theory, financial system, governmental structure, work of art, song, novel, TV show, movie, poem—the list goes on and on—is about trying to express and make sense of what can't be fully expressed or understood. Our efforts to understand life are good things, but none of them tell the full story. They can't adequately depict the glory of life or give us control over the heartache in it.

We are created to live fully—to imagine, to feel, to need, to desire, to long, to hope, to create, to succeed, to fail, to be hurt, to heal, and to imagine again. No matter how good life is or how difficult life becomes, we are created for more. Our hearts are made to live fully and free. As spiritual beings, we are made for so much more than we can ever experience in this life.

Addiction: An Illusion of Control

Because we are made to live life to the full, we will experience how painful life is. We are created to live full-heartedly, and that means life is going to hurt terribly. We live pushed and pulled between the truths that life is tragically difficult and life is incredibly glorious. We survive and thrive east of Eden and west of glory, between a place where we were created and a place where we will find our complete fullness and freedom.

We have two options: (1) live on life's terms or (2) attempt to control life. We are made for the first. We all do the latter. Each of us tries to create for ourselves a world in which we have control. Unfortunately, that world doesn't exist.

There is a reasonable part of us that wants to avoid a full life. We want to settle for a safe and happy life. Because we have experienced heartbreak (betrayal, abandonment, abuse, loss, trauma, neglect, and disappointment), we attempt to fashion lives that are smaller and manageable—or worse, foreclosed on completely. Or we attempt to make ourselves bigger than life. We ultimately, however, make ourselves worn out and burned out trying to create our own Edens—trying to maintain a predictable, pleasurable perfection.

Too often we turn our freedom to create toward developing mechanisms that we believe will deliver us from the reality and struggle of life. We want to avoid the emotional and spiritual impact of a difficult world.

This is where addiction enters the picture. This book will go much deeper into this, but for now, let's just say that *addiction occurs when our attempts to control life take control of us*. We try to create an internal emotional and spiritual haven that ends up becoming a prison. And because humans are so creative, the list of human addictions is endless. To paraphrase an REM song, life is bigger than us, and there is no length we will not go to find some sense of certainty or control.[1]

Painting a Picture of Hope

Throughout this book, we will touch on the emotional, spiritual, psychological, physiological, theological, and sociological aspects of addiction. Comprehensively covering something as massive, controversial, and complex as addiction in one book is impossible. We will not try in this book to synthesize the complexity and disparate views of addiction and its cures. Instead, we will paint a picture of hope by describing the following:

- the path we all take toward addiction
- the path we can walk to live in freedom from addiction
- the tools we need to live consistently in that freedom

Many of the people we have worked with over the years have made it out of the depths of despair and confusion to

29

live abundantly. You will read several stories of addiction in this book. They are written by real people but details have been changed for the sake of privacy. When anonymity is not preserved, it is at the request of the individual—most often because they work publicly in the world of addiction recovery.

A Story of Hope and Love

Addiction is a devastating pandemic that has its grip on the throat of the world. If you are reading this book, the odds are great that addiction is a part of your story—either in your life or in the life of someone you care deeply about. Addiction brings destruction, despair, and death, and its scars are everywhere. But even though this book is about a devastating pandemic, it is even more about the power of hope and courage. What evil intends for our harm, our God can use for our good.

More than a book about addiction, this is a book about a hope that is real, present, and active in the human heart and on the earth. It is also a book about love. Love is the center of it all. God is working to restore all things, and love is the most common and powerful tool. As you read about addiction, please keep heart and remember that you are a part of a story of hope and love.

You are loved.
Life is a struggle.
God is love.

PART 1

THE AGE OF ADDICTION

Aldous Huxley's novel *Brave New World* depicts a utopian society set in the futuristic World State in which the citizens are encouraged to take daily doses of the drug Soma. In small doses, Soma makes people feel good. In larger doses, it creates euphoric hallucinations and a sense of ecstasy. When citizens of the World State experience emotions, they take a Soma "holiday" to distract them from the unpleasant feelings. Huxley described the lengths humans will go in order to avoid the experience of being human.

In an example of life imitating art, Valium became the world's first blockbuster drug, "the first $100 million brand in pharmaceutical history, and between 1968 and 1981, the most widely prescribed medication in the Western world." At its peak sales, in "1978 alone, Valium's manufacturer, Hoffman-La Roche, sold nearly 2.3 billion tablets, enough to medicate half the globe."[1]

> Roche [a global pharmaceutical manufacturer] created the idea—and doctors bought it—that you can have better living through chemistry. They have created what Aldous Huxley

envisioned in *Brave New World*. They have given us soma, and it is called Valium.[2]

Valium was just the beginning. The explosive growth of psychopharmacology (the scientific study of the effects drugs have on mood, sensation, thinking, and behavior) in the second half of the twentieth century and the beginning of the twenty-first century has ushered in the "brave new world" in which much of the human experience is increasingly regulated, influenced, and controlled by pills. From feelings, thoughts, and personalities to sleep rhythms, sexual confidence, and hunger, the most elemental parts of being human can be managed by the pharmacy.

Our "brave new world" is not so brave. In our earnest attempts to help suffering people feel better, we have labeled much of the human experience as weakness or abnormal. In an attempt to cure this "sickness" of being human, we have normalized and institutionalized the numbing of the human heart. We expect our internal lives (our feelings, needs, desire, longings, and hopes) to feel manageable and comfortable. We all want an easy fix, and the snake oil salesman is always there with the magic elixir.

At its essence, this move by Western science is not new but merely a more scientific, modern, worldwide attempt to deal with an age-old issue. Humans of every generation and of every culture throughout history have wanted a "pill" that could lift them out of the daily struggle of what it means to be human. With rapid industrialization and technological advances, along with the secularism of our age, feeling comfortably numb has never been more accessible and permissible than it is now. It is no wonder that perhaps the greatest problem facing the world is addiction.

1

THE INVISIBLE DRAGON

There is an invisible dragon that wants to enslave your heart, enslave your will, and control your mind—it wants to devour you while you are alive. Everyone—child, adult, and elderly; rich, middle class, and poor; majority, minority, and marginalized; conservative, progressive, and moderate—is at risk. No matter who you are, where you're from, where you live, or what you know or believe, this monster seeks a way to get to you.

This beast is thousands and thousands of years old. It lives in the open. It can be found in every town, suburb, and city; every church, temple, and mosque; every tribe, culture, and race in every part of the world. It doesn't have to hide, and it takes on many shapes and forms. It is familiar to almost every person. The name of this dragon is addiction, and the world is under its spell.

While this may sound dramatic, like the beginning of a fantasy novel, calling addiction the invisible dragon is an apt metaphor for how this plague controls and damages the lives of far too many.

Hiding the Dragon: Denial and Dissociation

No one plans or wants to become addicted, and yet millions upon millions of us are, and we cannot face the dilemma in which we live. The dragon uses two survival gifts God has given us to hide in plain sight and build its power: denial and dissociation. For many of us, denial allows us to ignore what is happening so we can tolerate emotionally difficult situations. Similarly, dissociation allows us to block experiences that are emotionally overwhelming and over which we feel powerless. These defenses are necessary for people in families and cultures that don't support, admit, or permit emotional expression. Addiction piggybacks on these survival processes. Denial and dissociation are two defenses that addiction uses to stop us from seeing and feeling the consequences of what is happening in our lives.

Denial has five key characteristics that numb the heart and prime us for addiction.

1. Don't see. Ignore what is actually happening.
2. Don't feel. If we don't see, we won't have feelings that could render us vulnerable to rejection or humiliation or that could disrupt the status quo of survival. Tragically, these actions are thought of as "keeping the family together," "avoiding helplessness," and "being good."
3. Don't need. By not feeling, we don't have to need. Needs put us in a position of dependence on others who could potentially betray or abandon us.

4. Don't speak. When we ignore or deny our needs, we won't be tempted to talk about what is occurring inside of us. Expressing one's self (especially in impaired families or toxic institutional systems) can threaten to make things worse and put us and others in positions of being in "trouble" or being labeled as "difficult" or "causing trouble."

5. Don't trust. By not seeing, feeling, needing, or speaking, we become isolated and self-protective. We reject our internal experience and external reality in order to maintain the status quo.

The defenses that protected us from having to face and feel our emotional pain become habits that protect us from having to face and feel what is happening in our lives. For almost all addicts this practice of defenses begins in childhood long before they become addicted. The seed of addiction always begins in childhood. Addiction uses our childhood fear and shame of having feelings and needs to enslave us.

To stay blind to seeing addiction as the massive problem it is, we practice mantras that keep us from facing and feeling life's present and past experiences. These mantras sound like the following:

- "If your life was as hard as mine, you would _____ too."
- "The only time I get a break from stress is when I _____."
- "I'm just having a good time."
- "What happened to me wasn't that bad."
- "What doesn't kill me makes me stronger."

- "It's water under the bridge."
- "They did the best they could."
- "No one will ever understand."
- "If somebody finds out, no one will love me."
- "Next time it will be different."
- "Don't be sad that _____ is dead."
- "It was really my fault."
- "I should've known better."
- "God doesn't give anybody more than they can handle."

Staying blind to pain through denial is not enough. We also try to block the pain. During stressful/traumatic experiences, dissociation helps us deal with what is too difficult to bear. Dissociation is a reflexive ability to separate ourselves from the emotional experiences that are happening to or around us. In its mildest forms, it allows us to compartmentalize the emotionally difficult moments in order to come back and deal with them later. When there is no one to go to for emotional expression and relational connection, it becomes dissociation. In situations such as childhood sexual or physical abuse, the sudden death of a parent, rape, an accident, war, disaster, or being the victim of a crime, a child may reflexively dissociate the feelings, circumstances, or memories of the situation, thereby emotionally escaping from the shame, pain, or terror. This is especially true when a child has no one to go to for emotional healing.

Even as they try to protect us from the distress and trauma of life, denial and dissociation damage us all and suppress our ability to recover from addiction. Denial and dissociation isolate us from ourselves; they make emotional intimacy and vulnerability impossible between people. They separate us from the heart of God because we aren't present in heart to experience life. Addiction uses this isolation to increase its effect.

The heart-wrecking effects of distress and trauma out of which denial and dissociation develop as forms of protection aren't enough to keep the heart's cries silent—this requires something more potent. Most often the things that are powerful enough to quiet the heart also have the power to take control of us, decimate our relationships, destroy our lives, and kill us—and they do. There is a direct correlation between how effective a substance, behavior, or process is at creating emotional and spiritual illusions and how addictive it is. The greater the pain a person is in, the greater the need for relief. Sometimes that relief creates false realities. For example, when a person is going through a difficult divorce and facing the challenges of being a single parent, they can be in significant emotional and spiritual distress. By using a "pill" (either a substance or process), they can create a momentary illusion of well-being. The greater the distress, the stronger the attachment to the "pill" that created the comfort—though the comfort is only a momentary illusion.

Understandably, we all want to experience the very best of life while avoiding the very worst of life. We all want a way to feel alive and yet to keep life manageable by not being too surprised, emotionally vulnerable, or out of control. The dragon of addiction incubates in our attempts to manufacture internal experiences that are free of pain, anxiety, and shame. Emotionally and spiritually, addiction is an impaired attempt to find a full life without having to pay the price of feeling all that life requires us to feel.

Turning the Tide

There is real hope. Hearts can be healed. Denial can be dismantled. The numbness of dissociation can lift. Addiction can be defeated. But for these things to happen, we must be willing to name and face the ways we survive; turn from the denial we've practiced; daily lean away from the dissociation we've lived in; and be honest with ourselves, others, and God about the specific methods and substances we use to manufacture emotional and spiritual illusions. To be free of addiction's death grip, we must practice living life as vulnerable and resilient emotional and spiritual beings.

In Scripture, the first question God asked was the Hebrew word *Ayeka* (Gen. 3:9). The English translation is "Where are you?" but this translation doesn't capture the full meaning of the word. The question does not refer to geographical location. (God knew they were hiding among the trees.) *Ayeka* is a question of sorrow. It's a question of missing someone. It's a matter of the heart. God asked Adam and Eve, "Where are you? Tell me where your heart has gone." *Ayeka* invited Adam and Eve to speak from the heart in kind, expressing their true emotional condition.

Scripture goes on to say that Adam said, "I was afraid because I was naked; so I hid" (v. 10). Adam told the truth. He expressed the emotions of his heart, spoke the truth aloud, and handed himself back over to the processes of God. He became reattuned to relationship. God's heartache, *Ayeka*, invited Adam and Eve to feel, to tell the truth, and to give back the hearts they had tried to hide from God.

The aim of God's question was Adam's and Eve's hearts. It was a question to affect and change them, to enable Adam and Eve to return to themselves, to return to relationship with each other, and to return to intimacy with God.

God continues to ask us the same question today. Our answer to the question opens the door to beginning again. Instead of hiding out, we are called on to cry out. Therein lies the ancient doorway to liberation and, conversely, the answer to how we become enslaved.

GREG'S STORY OF HOPE

I was born in the Midwest on my own father's birthday. He was a physician completing his residency training. My mom was a nurse and the daughter of missionaries. My parents were married during their medical training. Both had dreams of becoming medical missionaries, and soon after my birth, those dreams were realized as they moved my older siblings and me overseas to serve. Another sibling was born soon after, and we lived with other foreign medical staff families while attending school.

My father worked constantly, as the needs were great for his medical expertise. My mom raised us and also worked with other kids. My parents were very strong in their faith and commitment to serve God, feeling called to this life by him. My father, however, suffered from health issues, and because of this, when I was ten years old, we returned to the States.

The experience of returning to middle-class America from a third world country was a pivotal time for my siblings and me. We felt awkward, different, like we were from outer space. Financially, socially, and academically, we were behind and different. We wore weird, outdated clothes. We were poor at that time with little to play with or show off. We didn't understand the little unspoken gestures and innuendos. We did not fit in, and it was confusing. My older siblings had a more difficult time making friends than I did, struggling with emotional stress, depression, and academics. I, on the other hand, did find some close friends in the neighborhood. Even though feeling a sense of embarrassment for being different, I had people to hang with. I spent more time away with friends, and in middle school, this increased. Three of us got to be close and stayed together all the way through high school.

These two friends came from strained home relationships, having both parents with difficult relationships and older siblings who exposed them to alcohol and drugs. We were around alcohol and drugs regularly, and soon, in middle school, my friends began to try them. I developed a familiarity with partying and such. We would smoke together from time to time and use oral tobacco. My friends would drink alcohol when they could find some. Early on, I resisted. My upbringing, faith, and convictions were important to me, but these friendships were even more so. I belonged, even with my differences.

Strangely, I also remained very involved in my church. I enjoyed youth activities and relationships there and became a leader in the high school group. But outside the church, I continued hanging out and partying with my other friends. Although feeling guilty at times and wanting things to be different, I continued to participate in these two different lifestyles. I soon was using alcohol nightly and smoking and using marijuana. While using these, I found something I was missing. I felt a part of something, a greater confidence socially, and a sense of being okay in my own skin. This would wear off the next day, and I would smoke and drink again.

Through the end of high school and into college, I continued this pattern of coping. I used alcohol primarily in a pattern of binging on weekends and such. This I did in secret with certain friends while keeping my reputation protected in the other areas of life. I was always chasing the buzz, looking for a sense of being okay. I never drank out of a love for the taste. It was a means to an end. Although feeling like a hypocrite, an imposter in many ways, and at times guilty over my actions, I continued.

I was able to do this while also doing well academically. I was very involved in college life and sports and extracurricular activities. I played soccer, sang in choir, served on student government, and led in other student positions. I knew I wanted to go to medical school, so I was careful to work hard. I was able to complete premed training, applied to medical school, and was accepted. I was on my way.

It was soon after this in my senior year that I would take a detour. Through a friend's influence on me, I had a spiritual experience that led me to consider going into the ministry instead of medical school. I gave up alcohol and my plans in order to pursue helping others. I deferred my medical school acceptance to take a year to explore this by working with kids in a large church program. Although it was a great year personally, it did not bring clear resolution. I ended up deciding to pursue medicine and so began medical school, when similar patterns of coping reappeared.

Despite ongoing external success, I was plagued with internal fear. Spiritually, my faith suffered. It was not enough. The work stress, fear of failure, and isolation grew. My solution was to achieve and work harder. I was unable to be honest and ask for help. I received affirmation from peers and faculty, but this did not fill the hole in me. I continued to fall back into drinking, often binging, on my own. Seeking relief, I would also attend church and pray but felt far from God.

It was during this time that I met a woman, and we started dating. Although we both fell for each other, I was unable to be honest with her. She believed in me early on, but I continued to sabotage the relationship. The relationship had its ups and downs, but eventually we got married and began our life together.

We moved to begin my residency in family medicine. During this three-year period, I continued the same patterns. I was personally mentored by the chair of the department. In retrospect, I realize that he saw something in me, both my potential and also my internal struggle. I see that I refused to be honest with him despite much opportunity. My fear of being exposed and looking weak or incapable was too strong. Therefore, I kept him at arm's length along with others.

In addition, loneliness in my marriage grew as I worked long hours and did not know how to be in relationship with my wife. We also experienced several difficulties, the worst of which was a miscarriage.

After completing my training, I joined a growing practice. We bought our first house, joined a church, and settled in. My life was immediately consumed with work that approached fourteen-hour days, including inpatient and outpatient care. Although enjoying my work and aggressively trying to be a good partner in the group and grow my practice, I began in the first year to be overwhelmed and stressed. This led to increased stress in our home. My wife became pregnant again, and we became more isolated from each other.

I was beginning to feel like I was a failure at home, at work, and with myself. I turned to drinking, first intermittently and then, within months, nightly in increasing amounts. I hid the amounts from my wife. I moved into more isolation. A sense of being overwhelmed grew deep within me. Everything was affected.

Conflicts with my wife increased as she became more and more lonely and concerned. I was unavailable, often leaving her alone with our young child. I was often too tired and stressed to be present even when I was there. I was crashing on the couch and passing out, unable to concentrate, and increasingly emotionally and spiritually numb. Alcohol seemed to help, or so I thought.

My faith and my connection to God suffered as I felt more and more a failure and unworthy of his love. I began to look for punishment and consequences from my choices. Prayer was more difficult with a sense of hopelessness. I would try to reconnect by quitting alcohol, confessing, working harder to do right, but change never was sustained. I would turn back to alcohol over and over again for relief. I tried friendships at church, but I was relationally unavailable and could not show up in them. Although drinking, I attempted to help lead small groups at church. I read the Bible and prayed, but all seemed powerless to help me change.

Soon I was using hydrocodone as well. I found that this gave me the same and even better sense of being okay without the side effects of alcohol—namely, hangovers. Using hydrocodone was also easier to hide. Although doing so was illegal, I began diverting drug prescriptions. I began using various pharmacies to obtain hydrocodone under different names. This became my obsession, and patients and family took second place.

After the birth of our second child, the downward spiral picked up quickly. Our baby had a severe illness in the neonatal period that resulted in her re-admission to the hospital. The fear and uncertainty of this led me to increase my drug use. Work, marriage, and parenting all suffered. Daily, I was impaired. I was more and more focused on obtaining narcotics and alcohol with care to avoid detection. In many ways, my wife had to do much of the decision making for and care of our children. I was never really there.

After trying to stop, I would return to using drugs again within a month. I got to a new low. I remember a sense of hopelessness, a sense that my life was a failure and that my wife and family would be better off with me gone. I hated myself. In an odd moment, I came to a place of willingness. While sitting in my office, I prayed a prayer I had intentionally avoided for years. I believed God would probably answer this one. It went something like this: "I need help. I can't ask anyone for help. If you bring someone to me, I will be honest and admit it." I knew immediately that the gig was up.

Within one hour, one of my physician partners knocked on my door and asked if he could speak to me. This discussion led to a conversation with the head of a physicians' advocacy and support program for an evaluation. After admitting to my wife some of the truth, I entered a treatment program for physicians. This changed the trajectory of my life and my family's life.

Through this prolonged treatment program, I began to wake up to the truth. I immediately felt relief. My first 12-step meeting in treatment was a Narcotics Anonymous meeting. A man was telling his story. He had lived on the streets in the drug-dealing world. I will never forget the clear sense that he was telling my story. We were so different, yet the feelings he described were mine too. I felt hope.

Through the next few weeks, I came to understand the reasons I did what I did, why the drugs and alcohol were so strong for me, why I kept going back to them. I began to see that these were not my true problem but a symptom of a deeper sickness. This deeper sickness was one of a belief of my own defectiveness, my own toxic shame, and a dysfunctional way of dealing with the feelings of fear, shame, and guilt. I had built a false self. I believed it was not okay to be me.

Through the treatment process, I began to gain a new freedom. I came to understand why I turned to drugs and alcohol to cope with life. I learned that it was not the drink or drug that was the problem but a broken person inside. In treatment, the vast majority of time was spent on understanding just this. In addition, I learned about the Spiritual Root System, my core feelings, why we have them, how they are a guide to what is going on inside, and what action I can and need to take. Doing treatment with others in the same process, I began to see myself in others, and I came to trust in how being honest with myself and others leads to healing and a fuller life. I learned how God shows up in truth with another.

During the next two years, I spent much time and energy going to Alcoholics Anonymous, attending counseling, and restoring my work relationships. My AA sponsor became a guide to the steps and their application to my life. I got to see how the stories of other recovering addicts and alcoholics help me in my new way of living. I had a place to bring my daily problems and fears. I returned to my same job but in a much more balanced way. Through the support of the program for impaired physicians, I had an advocate in my profession. I began to see patients and colleagues through a new lens, with more understanding, fewer comparisons, more accepting and compassion. How my practice benefited!

An area that needed help was my marriage and home life. The hopelessness my wife and I had experienced for years before treatment had caused much strife and pain. My lies, workaholism, abandonment, and resentment along with her loneliness and fear and our family stress had driven us apart and left us empty.

Through my treatment, we began to have hope for us. We participated in counseling on and off for a couple of years. We had to learn how to be in a healthy relationship and unlearn much dysfunction. I had used alcohol to cope at home as well. Now we began to rediscover our love, our friendship, and the things that drew us to each other in the first place.

Learning to be honest was so hard for me. My default was always self-protection. Just saying I would be late coming home because of a patient consult was so hard and new. Her challenge was to trust me again. She had little reason to believe my words. In time, one day at a time, we began to learn a new way of life. Healing continued. We began to bear things together. We began to talk about and carry together my stress from work, our children's struggles, our financial situation, and my wife's concerns.

It has been over seventeen years since I walked into treatment, at a bottom that had me completely hopeless. What are some things I have learned and experienced? Well, I am comfortable in my own skin most of the time. I know how to ask for help or give appropriate help. I have learned about intimacy and friendship with other men and have experienced the blessing of such. I feel more now, such as joy, sadness, loneliness. I see life as more tragic now, but with that I see its increased meaning and purpose. I see myself as belonging, no better or worse. I shoot for progress, not perfection. I am willing to ask for forgiveness and own my part in conflicts. I forgive myself more quickly. I hope for more. For all this, I am so grateful!

In addition, I am more accepting of where I am in life. I care more for people. I can say "no" more easily when needed. I understand boundaries. I can give and hold back more appropriately.

I see God as a pursuer, a lover of people, more giving and forgiving. He is bigger now. I believe he is in control.

My life is full. I have a full medical practice and get to mentor other physicians. I teach medical students and get to build into others principles I have learned from my experience. I choose to serve in areas that help people who are disenfranchised. I get to be in my kids' lives. I get to be involved with kids through church. I get to dream about the future and my next steps, not out of fear but out of calling.

What do I hope for in the future? More of this life! More surrender to God. More love for my wife and more time with her. More friendship, not with many but deeper with a few. More of my kids, relationship with them, more memories, more curiosity about them. More time. More reading and growing and thinking. To spend more time in service in ways that help those who can't help themselves. To enjoy life. To bring a message of hope to those I find around me. To live a truly sober life!

2

THE PANDEMIC

Scientists classify the widespread occurrence of disease using three general categories: outbreak, epidemic, and pandemic. An outbreak is when a disease occurs in greater numbers than expected in a community or region or during a season. An epidemic is when a disease rapidly spreads throughout a region. A pandemic is when a disease spreads beyond a region to other areas of the world.

- An outbreak is localized.
- An epidemic is a rapidly spreading regionalized disease outbreak.
- A pandemic is a global disease outbreak.

Pandemics are devastating to a population because a pandemic has no boundaries, no racial, ethnic, religious, age, geographic, or socioeconomic stopping point. A pandemic leaves no one immune.

It's not a stretch to understand addiction as a pandemic, but we tend to be in denial about and dissociate from what addiction is and how it operates. How can we do something about an illness that we don't see or accept as the sickness it is or when we don't acknowledge the impact it has? Addiction is destroying, overtly and covertly, millions of lives. No one person—child or adult—is unaffected by addiction. It's hard to think of something as abnormal when it's so common, and it's difficult to address something we don't adequately understand.

According to recent statistics gathered by the Substance Abuse and Mental Health Services Administration, 23.5 million Americans over the age of twelve are addicted to alcohol or illegal drugs.[1] That number does not include the millions of other Americans who are addicted to prescribed medications. The opioid epidemic, for example, according to Nora Volkow, director of the National Institute on Drug Abuse, has partially been caused by a "healthcare system that sought to minimize pain and suffering. Physicians were taught that those with pain wouldn't get addicted to pain medication." She goes on to say that "those beliefs were completely wrong."[2] As of this writing, Americans use 95 percent of the world's production of narcotics.[3] That same healthcare system overprescribes by the millions other profoundly addictive substances such as antianxiety and sleep medications. The healthcare system's temporary solutions can lead to long-term negative effects. In the United States, 130 people die every day from overdosing on opioids.[4]

In 2018, a pornography corporation that keeps its own data, Pornhub, stated that 33.5 billion visits to its sites occurred—on average, 92 million visits per day worldwide, and

962 searches per second. The pornhub.com site boasts, "If you were to start watching 2018's videos after the Wright brother's first flight in 1903, you would still be watching them today 115 years later!"[5] The sex industry holds millions of people in its grip through sex addiction, and the numbers are climbing. Pornhub is just one of many businesses operating in the sex industry.

In the United States, it is estimated that about 18 percent of men either think they are addicted or are unsure if they are addicted to pornography, which equates to 21 million men in America.[6] Surprising to many is that studies show the same is true for women—about 1 in 5 women (18 percent) use the internet for sexual purposes weekly.[7] That is about 17.7 million women. When we combine men and women, we find that about 38.7 million American adults use pornography regularly. This number doesn't include children or those adults who act out sexually in other ways.

In 2016, the North American Foundation for Gambling Addiction Help reported that approximately 2.6 percent of the US population has some type of gambling issue. That adds up to nearly 10 million people in the United States who struggle with a gambling habit.[8]

It is estimated that 8 million Americans have an eating disorder—7 million women and 1 million men.[9]

In total, approximately 25 percent of the US population has an active, recognized addiction.

- alcohol and illegal drugs: 23.5 million
- prescription drugs: 2 million
- pornography: 38.7 million
- gambling: 10 million

- eating disorders: 8 million
- total: 82.2 million

Millions of people also struggle with other addictions such as work addiction disorders or power, appearance, exercise, perfectionism, anxiety, and other process addictions. Process addictions are compulsive behaviors that don't directly include substance. When these addictions are thrown into the mix with the big three of alcohol, drugs, and sex, the numbers are staggering.

Everyone in America is touched by addiction. Speaking only of the 23.5 million alcohol and drug addicts (saying "only" about 23.5 million people seems absurd), research indicates that for every person addicted to alcohol or drugs, three to four people in relationship with the addict experience life-damaging effects. Any person connected for an extended period with someone who has an addiction will suffer some of the characteristics of post-traumatic stress. Predominantly, family members and friends directly suffer the emotional and relational, if not the physical and financial, impact of addiction.

By multiplying 23.5 million alcohol and drug addicts times the minimum number of three people impacted by their addiction, we find that 70.5 million people are harmed emotionally and relationally by people trapped in their own emotional and relational maelstrom of addiction. Adding the 23.5 million addicted sufferers to the 70.5 million people affected by their addiction reveals the power of addiction and its devastating consequences. Ninety-four million Americans are presently suffering emotional and relational distortions, distress, and distrust—all connected to this one common denominator of alcohol and drugs alone. Ninety-four million Americans are in acute distress, hidden behind walls of denial and dissociation.

The number of those affected by addiction expands exponentially when we begin to consider the impact of all the other addictions. Addiction of any kind harms the addict and those connected to them. Addiction takes away a person's capacity for emotional and spiritual connection, intimacy, and love, which detrimentally impacts those in relationship with them. It sets a person up to disconnect from their own emotional and spiritual being. Addiction and its impact are America's number one internal problem. But the pandemic is everywhere.

The addiction pandemic is an emotional, spiritual, and relational crisis of massive proportions. We are in the midst of a pandemic that symptomatically, destructively affects our minds, hearts, and bodies. It has infected our families, friends, and neighbors. It is eroding our ethics, morality, culture, and economy. It threatens to shred the woven fabric that connects us all—to ourselves, to one another, and to God.

No matter how much we attempt to address our personal, family, community, national, and global problems without dealing with addiction, we will fail. As we individually accept responsibility for our addictions, we can all be a part of the solution for the addiction pandemic of our age. We can return our hearts to the God who desires to do for us what we cannot do for ourselves.

RACHEL'S STORY OF HOPE

It was a hellish decade. That's the only way to describe living in a godless marriage, being in deep denial of my own multitude of issues, and watching my husband's life unravel at the seams from addiction. Oh, and being in denial about that too. I didn't know anything about recovery, boundaries, or self-care. I had been taught to shake it off, endure, and live in secrecy. I had no idea what feelings were or how to feel them. I was about to embark on a long journey with no equipment, no guide, and no emotional strength to survive it.

It took thirty years of tribulations to get to this point. I grew up in an alcoholic, broken, and "Christian" home. Alcoholic, I would find out, because my parents grew up in alcoholic homes and had no recovery for themselves. Broken because of infidelity, lack of love and heart, and eventually divorce. "Christian" because we were at church every time the doors opened but never talked about God and were not taught about a relationship with Jesus. I was the victim of verbal and emotional abuse and knew all about abandonment.

Addiction was widespread on both sides of my family and would later lead to the truths about this way of life. Some would die, others would spend time in jail, and the crazy ones are still at it today. My female role models endured mental, physical, and sexual abuse. They medicated with alcohol and drugs, gossip, and a sense of status in their communities. They thought that the right cars, clothes, and houses would hide the truth about what was behind their front doors. These women would hang on for dear life to the things that were ruining theirs. The men they had vowed to love, honor, and cherish would be the objects of their own addiction, and they would sacrifice everything to stay with them. This was it! This was how marriage was done. Endurance worked. I had seen it my whole life.

My father was unfaithful. He finally confessed that he didn't love my mother and left at the end of my freshman year of high school. There was no real closure and no conversation with my parents about their divorce. At times it was like they were still married and living under different roofs. I do believe my mother would have stayed in their marriage forever. She would have endured the hurt and shame of not being loved to avoid being alone. Unfortunately, I absorbed this truth into my own thinking. I also held on to the untruth that I wasn't enough for my father to stay. His leaving cracked my heart wide open and began to expose the deepest parts to many untruths to come.

The pain of divorce was unbearable. I turned to alcohol, cigarettes, and sometimes boys. I used harmful things to numb the pain. I started failing in school, stopped going to church, and rejected anything healthy or good for me. I carried the shame of my failures and bad behavior and being one of the only kids from a broken home like a boulder on my back. I rejected the friendship of the local Young Life leader because if her Jesus was the one who was dictating my story, I was better off alone. My friends were orphans just like me, and we would raise each other until we got to escape to college.

I made many vows during my life, the first one being that I would never be the one to break up my own family. I would never put my children through what I'd experienced and would never be responsible for inflicting on them the pain of loss and abandonment. How could I have been so naive to think I had this power? I was that naive and believed I was that powerful, and so started thinking that I could control my world. I could manipulate others, alter myself, and endure anything to create the fairy-tale life that I wanted and deserved.

There were other vows. The most impactful vow was to marry a certain boy who had captured my heart in my early teens. I would go on to suffer through high school and eventually go to college, where depression and anxiety became major players in my life. I dated several guys, one seriously, but my heart belonged to someone else. He was a wild-at-heart rebel who was always ready for the next risky adventure. He was crazy smart, so handsome, and just plain charming. We started dating in our early twenties and married a few years later.

Dating for us was volatile. We had moved to a different city. We were far from home, family, and friends. We were angry and scared and running from our pain. We were playing house and using the only tools and methods that we knew existed. We didn't choose God but made each other God and were constantly disappointed. We drank hard, fought hard, and never considered there was a better way to live this life.

Marriage was going to fix everything. We had a fairy-tale wedding with warning signs of trouble to come. I have always believed that my husband got high outside the church "and didn't have a chance" to read the two-page letter I had written to him. I made the mistake of asking him if he read it while we were standing at the altar and quickly received the message that other things were more important than me.

My husband had a great job and was climbing the ladder quickly. I had a so-so job and didn't aspire to succeed in the workplace because having a family was on my mind. My mother stayed home with us, and I never considered anything different. Surely a baby would fill the void in my life, as it felt to me like my husband's job was quickly becoming his mistress.

Pregnancy didn't come easy, and the next several years were filled with sadness, disappointment, and fear. I could not get pregnant and would later discover that my fertility issues were causing the problem. We met with a fertility specialist, and I felt so much shame when my husband wrote active marijuana user on the doctor's questionnaire and was asked about it at our first appointment. We went on to have two beautiful children.

As my husband continued to climb the corporate ladder, I became lonelier and more fearful of what the future would bring. He started traveling quite a bit and eventually did a three-month stint in a foreign country. I was pregnant with our second child and struggling to keep it together. He was a mess when he got back and started his love affair with cocaine shortly after our second child was born. He lost his job, and the terrible decade began.

My faith was at an all-time low. How was I going to fix my life? How was I going to fix my husband's drug problem? I wasn't! The God I had rejected for so long had gone before me. He had appointed people to love and care for me, my husband, and my kids. He had written a story that only I would be able to tell.

The summer before I learned of my husband's cocaine problem, I saw an old friend on a downtown street. She hugged me so tightly and told me she had been praying for me for two years. God had put my brokenness on her heart, and she had been prayerfully lifting me up on a regular basis. She then pulled a copy of *Streams in the Desert* out of her purse and gave it to me. She explained that this book had saved her life as she had lived through the addiction problems of her first husband and son. I read this daily devotional without fail, and I would go on to share it with others just as she had done with me.

More amazing women had hugely impactful roles in my story. An acquaintance put me in touch with a new therapist friend of hers. This therapist became a lifeline for me. She knew all about the addiction world and guided me through the next several years. She was instrumental in getting my husband into his first and third rehabs. She also taught me that my own recovery was necessary, as addiction is a family disease.

As my life fell apart, God had a plan to pick up the pieces and put me back together with a new heart for him. My unraveling would include an eating disorder, filing for divorce, two visits to my gynecologist for STD/AIDS testing, and enough tears to fill a large bucket.

My husband's addiction was spiraling out of control. Life was filled with daily fears and disappointments. While cocaine was his drug of choice for a couple of years, he also used gambling, pills, and women to fill the bottomless hole in his heart. He missed performances at school, acted crazy at sporting events, and spent almost all the money we had. I constantly reminded myself that addiction was a disease and that he wasn't intentionally trying to ruin my life. I also clung to that vow that I wouldn't be the one to destroy our family even though I knew in my heart that only an insane person would stay in this situation. I wasn't crazy. I was tough, and I had been taught how to endure this marriage. It would take many years and lots of hard work to break down the tough-girl facade I had created and to bust up the wall I had built around my broken heart.

My recovery continued to progress as I attended Al-Anon, joined grief and process groups, went to individual therapy, and dug into books and literature about recovery and how to live in a new and authentic way. I also opened my heart to new friends and became vulnerable with my story and the secrets I had kept for so long. My husband's recovery ebbed and flowed, and his arrest finally landed him in a program that literally saved his life.

The program lasted for three months. He lived in an apartment with other program members and was limited to almost no contact with his family. I was finished! I could not live this life for one more second. I agreed to let him complete the program before I made any life-altering decisions, but I knew the end of my marriage was near. My children were broken, and I was messing them up in ways I didn't even realize. I was teaching my daughter to keep secrets and expected her to act older and more responsible than her years would allow. She had already lived through so much, and unfortunately, our recovery started after much damage had been done.

My husband's recovery program was miraculous. The program was led by men who loved God. They had dedicated their lives to helping men uncover the pain that had opened the door to addiction. They taught men how to live an authentic and honorable life. They taught them how to start living life fully. Over the next few months, I would learn many truths about my husband's life. I would sit for hours and talk with him, cry with him, and slowly start to forgive him. Our recovery as a family was starting, and it wasn't my vow that caused me to stay but a change of heart that could come only from the amazing grace of God.

I am full of gratitude today. As crazy as it sounds, I'm grateful for my story. At times it was not a story but a nightmare, but without it, I wouldn't be who I am today. I'm a devoted wife of more than two decades, a good enough mother, a faithful friend, a loving daughter and sister, and a woman in recovery. A year and a half after my husband got sober, I fell apart. The boulder I had been carrying finally broke my back. God blessed me with a new therapist who helped me define every broken piece of my heart and accompanied God with the rebuild. I had no choice but to continue to dig deep, trust others, and keep talking. The Swiss psychiatrist Carl Jung said, "Who looks inside, awakes." My husband's addiction put me in a place where I had to look inside, and today I am grateful to be awake.

3

THE EMOTIONAL AND RELATIONAL COSTS OF ADDICTION

The awful reality of addiction is that it doesn't destroy just the addict; it damages those in relationship with the addict. Addiction is contagious. Everyone involved is infected. For every person addicted, three to four people in relationship with the addict experience life-damaging, long-term effects.

Family members and close friends of addicts always directly suffer the devastating effects of addiction. And because addiction is progressive, the longer a person is in relationship with an addict, the greater the damage. The more deeply we love someone who is in addiction, the more we are harmed by addiction. Emotionally and psychologically, any person who is in relationship with an addict for an extended time will suffer some characteristics of post-traumatic stress.

The effects of addiction on loved ones are multifaceted. For example, financially, addiction often makes maintaining healthy finances impossible. Addiction costs are insidious, often creeping into personal finances without notice. This makes us less likely to realize how damaging the financial impact of an addiction is until it's too late. The price tag of buying an addictive substance or engaging in addictive behaviors (like shopping and gambling) isn't the only cost of addiction. There are other financial costs, such as increased medical bills, increased insurance premiums, legal bills, and a loss of income due to those involved not being able to work.

However, money is the smallest cost. By far, the biggest costs associated with addiction are emotional and relational. Being in a secure relationship with someone with an addiction is impossible. An addict's family members and friends live in a relationship that can be rife with anxiety, secrecy, loss, conflict, violence, emotional chaos, unspoken rules, scripts, shame, and fear. Only their own denial and dissociation make maintaining the relationship with the addict possible.

Children of Addiction

Addiction affects everyone who lives with it, especially the family and most profoundly the children. Rather than the family being able to grow in healthy patterns of flexibility while maintaining boundaries and values, the family system is controlled by the addiction. Instead of developing a foundation of expression of feelings, needs, desire, longings, and hopes, the addicted family builds a foundation of denial and secrecy. Upon that foundation, roles and rules are formed that use a script. Every word in the script and every action by the actors deny that there is a problem. The actions are a survival reaction to get needs of belonging, mattering, and security met while also maintaining the status quo of not making the addict worse.

A child who lives with a parent who is mood altered, preoccupied with their own anxiety and comfort, or spending significant amounts of time recovering from the effects of their addiction will miss the opportunities to foster healthy, secure attachment.[1] Adolescents and young adults who have an addicted or emotionally impaired parent are far more self-critical and less confident. This is especially true for daughters, while sons often feel less connected. It doesn't matter if the impaired parent is a dad or a mom. A child who grows up with a parent in addiction feels shame for who they are, and they are emotionally disconnected from their peers.[2]

When children experience trauma, they inevitably react by hiding their hearts. They resist the vulnerability needed for emotional expression, and they become incapable of relational intimacy.

Children affected by addiction believe they have to perform to have worth or acceptance. They develop distortions, distress, and distrust concerning their own sense of self-worth and their own sense of belonging and mattering. More simply put, they believe they have to earn love and rarely allow themselves to truly trust love when it's given. The tragic irony is that parents trapped in addiction suffer from the same internal struggles as their children.

No matter what the children achieve, how "good" they act, or how religiously faithful they become, none of their success, generosity, or piety will make them feel confident in themselves, secure with others, or safe with God. The watchful eye of hypervigilance is always present, driven by insecurity and the need to perform.

These children grow up with an internal sense of incompletion, and they fear they will never be enough. They want a full and vibrant relational life, but they lack the foundational know-how of what is required to live that life.

Family Roles in Addiction

The five characteristics of denial (I don't see, feel, need, speak, or trust) are the basic survival mechanisms that all family members practice as a way to survive the stranglehold of addiction. The invisible dragon turns everyone into a puppet, and every member acts and reacts according to its manipulations.

Addict. The person who is obviously the sickest in the family, the addict, has the most power and influence over the other family members. Their power is rooted, ironically, in the need others have to be connected to and loved by the addict. Because the addict is least available for relationship, those connected to the addict bend themselves into roles to try to get what they want and make the family "work." Each person in the family either overfunctions or underfunctions in service to the addict.

Enabler. Often the spouse of the addict, the second most powerful person is the enabler, who "teaches" other family members how to manage the person who has the addiction. Rules are established to maintain the status quo, and everyone in the family does whatever is necessary not to rock the boat.

Other roles. To follow the rules, children play roles in the family. Roles vary and blend, but they usually become fixed. Some examples include the following:

Hero. The hero brings acclaim to the family yet feels fear and inadequacy underneath their brave exterior. Versions of this role in a family include the saint, the athlete, and the performer.

Scapegoat. The scapegoat takes attention away from the addict by becoming a "problem" or a "rebel" the family members can focus on instead of the addict. The scapegoat feels ashamed and excluded, often finding worth in peer groups as a substitute for family.

Lost child. The lost child is the one no one seems to worry about. They stay out of the way, hiding their fear behind a veil of invisibility.

Mascot. The mascot brings laughter to the family and plays the role of distracter. This person is not taken seriously and is significant by being okay. They feel shame and fear.

These roles are only examples. There are as many roles as there are capacities to survive. However, the roles taken on by family members become fixed as each person performs their part as a way to keep the family together and suppress anything that could expose the family to helplessness and shame. Everything is about suppressing anxiety by maintaining denial and keeping the secret that "we are in trouble and don't know what to do but survive."

How Addiction Emotionally Impacts Others

Addiction takes control of the addict and those closest to them. Those who love the addict intuitively know that the addict is powerless to choose the relationship over the addiction. This is a terribly painful reality to face. In order to preserve the relationship, those in relationship with the addict have to find ways to shut down their own feelings and needs. The addiction becomes the focus of everything in the relationship. The closer a person is to the addict, the harder it is for them to see and do something different. Maintaining the status quo is the goal. Addiction is like a slowly sinking ship, and instead of climbing into a lifeboat, those in relationship with the addict continue bailing water.

Family members and friends face an awful choice: disrupt the status quo (which means emotional pain and possibly the end of the relationship) or maintain the status quo and survive by serving the addiction. To avoid this awful choice, those in relationship with the addict have to practice their own denial and dissociation (just like the addict). Denial and dissociation become the foundation on which the relationship stands. Like the addict, family members and friends become slaves to the addiction. They unknowingly become enablers in service to sickness.

Loss of Freedom in Service to Sickness

Human beings are born with five freedoms. These freedoms help us belong and matter in healthy ways when they are affirmed and confirmed. The freedoms are as follows:

1. to say what I see
2. to say what I feel

3. to say what I need
4. to imagine myself in a positive future
5. to trust that others care about these expressions

Addiction robs us of these freedoms. Being in a relationship with an addict means we have to stay disconnected from these freedoms through denial and dissociation. We have to live by rules that keep us from how God created us and that disconnect us from living authentically in relationship. Here are the rules:

1. I don't say what I see, so that
2. I will not have to discover or expose what I feel, so that
3. I don't end up being in need.
4. I don't imagine myself in a full life but concentrate on survival and success as things that protect me more than they express who I am.
5. I don't trust that others care about what I see, feel, need, or imagine related to my true Self. (Your true Self is the imago Dei you carry—the image of God—in which each of us are uniquely created.)

Being controlled by addiction keeps us from seeing what is happening around us, and it keeps us from the lives we are made to have. We can't be who we are made to be. In the name of love, we end up sacrificing our freedom and well-being on the altar of addiction.

MARK'S STORY OF HOPE

I grew up in a family of prestige because my father was a significant figure in our city. We lived on over one hundred acres, raised cattle, and had a pool and a tennis court.

My father grew up on a farm outside of town, made it through graduate school, was asked to stay and teach, but returned to his roots. He went back home to help improve his city, to prove himself, and to heal his pain.

I remember many of his childhood stories. He walked behind a plow and mules to turn the ground for the next planting; they didn't have a tractor until he was in college. He wired their home for electricity when he was in college. He also talked about feeling inferior as a poor boy from the country who went to the town school. I recall feeling bad for him and ashamed of myself because of how easy I seemed to have it.

He overcame his outward circumstances and was adored by the thousands of people he had helped. He did not, however, lose his inward pain and shame. He healed many; he did not get healing for himself.

I was eleven years old when the symptoms of drug addiction began to show in my father. He fell asleep at the wrong times, needed to go to his office at odd hours, and had a barely concealed seething and anxiety in him that made me careful when with him. I didn't want to bother him. I acted as normal as possible around him, but inside I was uneasy. I felt somehow that my presence irritated him.

The script my siblings and I learned said that he was exhausted from all the demands put on him because of his profession, and we conformed our roles according to that script. Though there was some truth to it, the fact is he had become addicted to drugs.

The myth about his actions was that they were caused by stresses at work. The truth about his actions was that they were caused by addiction. We went with the myth. We acted, played our roles, and followed the rules my mother taught us. By maintaining the status quo, we had a sense of normalcy. To face addiction meant helplessness. We had no tools for helplessness or neediness. The addiction was a secret, and denial kept the secret where secrets are kept—in the dark.

Before the addiction began, I was just scared of him. He was strong, big, tough, important, tired, and gone most days and nights helping others. I knew at an early age that I was not strong, smart, or important like he was. Everything about me was childish; everything about him was significant.

My siblings and I had separate lives from him. One life when he was at home—quiet and careful. My mother saw to that. Another life when he wasn't home—playful and rambunctious. My mother enabled that. She loved him, and that love translated into controlling the environment to make everything seem okay. Without words, she taught us how to act when he was home.

We had two lives before the addiction. Perhaps we were already practicing for what was coming. Addiction to work rarely seems like real addiction, but it is. We were already growing up in an abnormal family before it became worse. To the outside world, we looked great. We knew perfectly well to honor the appearances. But behind the front door, another world existed.

My siblings and I knew how to follow the script, play our fixed roles based on unwritten rules, and "read" our father's moods as we took cues from my mother's enabling. Everything was about surviving addiction by, ironically, doing everything possible to hide it—from each other and from all others. Maintaining the status quo was the number one unwritten rule.

One night in my midteens, the entire family was at the dinner table. My father sat in his chair at the head of the table. No one ever sat in his chair, even when he wasn't there. I sat to his left. My mother sat to his right. My siblings sat on either side of us.

My father had been working on farm projects all day on his day off. I had come in from football practice. We had already fed the cows, and we sat down to eat. My father looked particularly worn out. He was barely present. His eyes were glazed. One of his eyes seemed to drift off center, but not one of us said a word. We were all pretending that everything was normal.

We were acting like always when I saw him lift his fork with rice on it and then stop midway between his plate and his mouth, frozen. I remember, as in slow motion, a piece of rice falling from his fork and landing on his plate. I looked at my mother who was looking straight at me. Her face turned pale, then red, then back to normal skin tone in seconds. I "read her mind," telling me to do something.

I looked at my father, whose eyes had completely glazed over. His right eye had moved to the right and his left eye had moved to the left in a terrifying way. His hand remained frozen in midair. No one said a word. I reached out with my right hand and touched his shoulder and said, "You must be exhausted."

His hand went down, he slumped in his chair, and then he passed out, with his head hanging to one side. My sister shoved her chair away from the table and left, retreating to her room where she spent lots of time alone reading. The rest of us finished the meal. "My father was exhausted from all his hard work, even working the farm on his day off, while we enjoyed the fruits of his labor" was the line of denial that protected the addiction and reinforced our shame, though we thought we were protecting the family. Our shame was that we could never do enough to help him.

After the meal, we helped our mother clean the dishes. She finished cleaning up the kitchen. My youngest brother and I watched TV in the next room, while I kept one ear open for anything else in the kitchen. Another brother left to go somewhere with his friends. We all left my father "sleeping" at the table. My mother went to another room.

Later that night, I put my youngest brother to bed by watching a TV show called MASH that he and I watched every night. It comforted me too. My other brother came in later, red-eyed, to tell us good night. (He and his friends had already found marijuana.)

No one said a word about what had happened. No one said a word about all the other things that happened either. The family was coming apart, and the individuals in it were too. But the secret was kept, and denial continued to rule all the days and nights that followed until I was in my twenties.

Instead of my family developing around a foundation of connection, we orbited around secrets and denial. Our roles were cast, and we played our parts like actors reading a script. Every word in the script and every action by the actors were to support the denial that the problem was addiction. We loved each other and wanted to belong to each other, so we all tried to make it work.

The disease of addiction is a contagious sickness. It affects everyone it touches, especially the family and most profoundly the children. Rather than my family being able to grow in healthy ways, our family system was controlled by the addiction.

Finally, through intervention, my father went to treatment for five months. We were surprised to learn that he was addicted to drugs, even though the evidence had been there for many years. We believed that he was exhausted and had become deeply depressed.

Today, many decades later, I can see how my father's recovery helped heal our family and the families of many, many others. At my father's funeral visitation several years ago, there was a line out the door of our church of hundreds of people waiting to offer their condolences—many of those people with testimonies about how his sobriety helped them find healing and recovery.

I entered recovery several years after my father when my own life became unmanageable due to addiction. My siblings and I are close now. We love each other. We talk often.

PART 2

UNDERSTANDING
ADDICTION

If you have ever driven along the interstates in the southeastern United States, you may have noticed kudzu. This climbing, coiling, and trailing perennial vine was first introduced to the United States in 1876—and it has been swallowing the countryside at the rate of about fifty thousand baseball fields a year. Each vine grows about one foot per day (sixty feet per growing season). Today in the United States, kudzu occupies more than an estimated 7.4 million acres.

The great kudzu invasion wasn't intentional. It started out with well-meaning efforts to stop soil erosion in Pennsylvania. The plant was then used in the southeast to provide shade to homes and as an ornamental species. It is a tough and resilient plant that can survive during droughts when native plants can't. But kudzu is extremely bad for the ecosystems it invades because it smothers other plants and trees under a blanket of leaves, keeping them in its shade. It also contributes to accelerating climate change because it keeps the soil from retaining carbon.

Kudzu is a great metaphor for addiction. Like kudzu, addiction finds a way to spread, and when it takes root, it can envelop all areas of our lives until it ultimately kills us. In the early stages of addiction, we don't understand what we are doing, and we can't see where we are headed. Like kudzu, all addictions begin as a good idea.

The alcoholic may want to feel like they belong and matter.

The sex/romance/love addict may want to feel delighted in.

The cannabis addict may want to feel less worried.

The opioid addict may want to feel more comfortable.

The codependent person may want to feel like they care and are cared for.

The anxiety addict may want to feel safe.

The depression addict may want to stop hurting.

The Netflix addict may want to ignore the flashes of traumatic memories.

The social media addict may want to feel connected.

The shopping addict may want to be distracted.

The food addict may want to feel in control.

The workaholic may want to feel successful.

The exercise addict may want to feel powerful.

The religious addict may want to be sure God loves them.

The video game addict may want to feel adventurous.

The sports addict may want to be part of something bigger and exciting.

The addictive substance or behavior can take many forms. The relief it offers centers around emotion, even though it may comfort us physically, psychologically, relationally, and even spiritually. Before it infests our lives, addiction takes root in our earnest bids to make our emotional worlds comfortable and untroubled. Once the process of addiction takes over, what was, in the beginning, our naive attempts to make life less painful end up costing us everything emotionally and relationally. Addiction begins as an attempt to make heaven on earth or to escape how the world is. It becomes a life of pretending and misery. Our attempts to be free of trouble lead us to slavery.

4

WHAT IS ADDICTION?

No one sets out to be addicted. No one wakes up one morning and says to themselves in the mirror, "I think today I'm going to slowly destroy my life, my relationships, my career, and my heart." No one chooses addiction.

Not the stressed-out minister, dad of twin boys, Little League coach who hurt his back in a car accident and became dependent on hydrocodone. He never intended to find himself stealing meds from his sick parishioners when making pastoral home visits.

Not the ER doc who on more days off than not drinks a bottle of wine (or two) while she watches Netflix on her iPad until she "falls asleep"—her newlywed husband beside her channel surfing ESPN, ESPN2, ESPNU, the Golf Channel, and FS1.

Not the high school football coach who carries the shame of being sexually abused by his own coach years earlier. Now he smokes pot every morning before going to school and every evening when he sits alone in his apartment.

Not the affable grandmother of seven grandkids who even though diagnosed with type 2 diabetes still drinks sweet tea with every meal. She lives on a carbohydrate-based diet and eats a bowl of ice cream each night before bed.

Not the single mom who, after dropping her kids off at school, works all day at a call center. She then rushes home to make them dinner and get them to bed so she can log in to finish her online college degree while using her son's Adderall and vaping nicotine so she can stay "focused."

Not the twenty-four-year-old missionary in Uganda who spends hours each night on the internet binging on pornography and thinks, *If I just served God faithfully, this lust would go away.*

Not the fourteen-year-old high school freshman who devolves into tears, rage, and apathy when her parents ask her to leave her phone at home for a weekend family trip.

Not the fifty-seven-year old tenured literature professor who finds himself in a prison rehab unit detoxing from heroin.

Not the nineteen-year-old college sophomore who lost his scholarship and was expelled from an elite college because he spent more time in his dorm room playing video games than he did in class.

The examples are endless. Addiction does not discriminate. People of every race, faith, income level, profession, intellect, and age can become trapped in its grip.

Addiction is not a lack of willpower. Many addicts are extremely driven, determined, and accomplished people. And they have earnestly tried hard to quit, have promised to quit tomorrow, yet tomorrow just doesn't come.

Addiction is not a lack of intellect. Plenty of addicts are doctors, professors, pharmacists, scientists, writers, and theologians.

Addiction is not a lack of morality. Addicts are just as aware of right and wrong as anybody. There are as many kind, generous, compassionate addicts as there are jerks. Many addicts are some of the most dedicated servants of society, such as pastors, doctors, nurses, therapists, teachers, EMTs, firefighters, and law enforcement officers.

The tools of willpower, intellect, and morality that work to solve so many of life's problems are not the answer to the power and pain of addiction. (They can actually help fuel it.) These tools can assist a person in recovery, but they are not the solutions.

Devoted, Given Over, Enslaved

The word *addiction* means "to be devoted to or to give one's self over to something completely." The word *addiction* comes from the Latin word *addictus*, which means "to sacrifice, sell out, betray, and abandon." Those who are addicted have betrayed themselves and sold themselves in an attempt to find a way to avoid the pain of being human. This "deal" addicts cut with themselves to abandon how they are made frequently ends up in physical, psychological, emotional, and spiritual enslavement. No one volunteers for slavery—whether enslavement to approval seeking or performance, to smartphones or anxiety, to narcotics prescribed by a physician or heroin purchased in back alleys.

The Components of Addiction

Addiction is rooted in three very interrelated but distinct, powerful processes:

- physical
- psychological
- emotional and spiritual

This is what makes addiction so powerful, dangerous, deadly, and difficult to address. It isn't just physical. It isn't just psychological. It isn't just emotional and spiritual. Addiction affects, alters, and impairs a person in all three areas. However, it always begins as a way to escape discomfort or distress.

Physical

Addiction is an impairment that becomes a horrific sickness. Over time our bodies and brains become physically dependent on these relief-seeking mechanisms. Consider the withdrawal effects of something as ineffectively mood altering as sugar or caffeine: headaches, irritability, cravings, mood swings. Physically, some addictions are so dangerous to stop that withdrawal without medical care can kill the addict.

In 1957, the American Medical Association classified addiction as a disease. A disease is a morbid process, of known or unknown origin, that has a characteristic chain of symptoms that are progressive, chronic, at times acute, and often fatal. Acceptance of the disease model took hold because scientists were able to show that drugs physically alter the brain. Labeling addiction as a disease was extremely helpful, and doing so helped to destigmatize addiction. The disease model redefined addiction as more than a moral failure and opened doors for those wanting healing and recovery like never before.

In recent years, neuroscience has expanded our understanding of the physical side of addiction. One way we have come to understand addiction is as the unintended consequence of the brain doing what it is supposed to do: seek pleasure and relief in a world that is painful and unpredictable.

Physically, the brain is made up of individual cells called neurons. Neurons are connected to one another by synapses. These connections have great capacity for change and adaptation—especially when we experience anxiety, pain, rejection, or shame. We are created to find well-being through connection in relationship. If we don't find it relationally, the brain hunts for the experience of connection elsewhere.

Neuroscience has revealed that in very primal and rudimentary ways, our brains will say yes to anything that relieves us of anxiety, pain, rejection, or humiliation. If these negative experiences are replaced with any sense of well-being, then the brain says yes! The brain quickly becomes conditioned to seek that experience again. The more uncomfortable our negative experiences, and the more efficiently and effectively they are replaced with relief and comfort, the more durable the synaptic pathway becomes. The brain is created by God to hunt for what satisfies it.

The more often this connection between distress and relief or pleasure plays out, the more our brains crave and seek the thing that brings relief or pleasure. Over time our entire world begins to revolve solely around the object of our desire. We become consumed by the quest for the next "hit."

The part of the brain that drives addiction, the limbic system, cannot discriminate whether the relief it seeks is ultimately good for us or bad for us. We engage in what neuroscientist and former addict Marc Lewis calls "motivated repetition." We repeat a pleasurable act, and our brains change in response. The more meaningful the act, the more effective the change in the brain. The momentum builds, "digging their own ruts—rainwater in the garden."[1] The compulsive nature of addiction occurs because all mood-altering substances or actions affect the brain's feeling center (the limbic system). In the brain, mood-altering substances and actions create durable and effective neurological pathways that mimic secure relational connections and personal accomplishment.

Psychological

It is currently in vogue to reduce addiction to merely brain biology. This is an unhelpful and ultimately dangerous course because it addresses only part of the problem. Another key component of addiction is psychological. Our psychology is how we make meaning of life.

The brain (the visible, tangible organ in the body) and the mind (the invisible, transcendent world of thought, attitude, belief, imagination, memory, dreams, and consciousness) are most often in tension with each other. Our brains crave pleasure. Our minds work to make meaning. Pleasure and meaning are more often than not in conflict. Pleasure comes through satiation, comfort, and control, whereas meaningfulness comes through relational connection, struggle, and resilience.

Humans are meaning-making creatures. The meaning we make is based on our experiences, beliefs, values, and cultural worldviews. We take action to express those things. What we buy (or don't). What we wear (or don't). The music we listen to (or don't). Much of our energy in life is spent consciously (aware) and unconsciously (unaware) expressing the story we want our lives to tell and reinforcing the narratives we hold most dear.

We are created with deep longings for justice, peace, rest, and safety. The conflict is that we live in a tragic world that keeps these longings from being completely fulfilled. Our world, while wonderful at times, is heartbreaking, lonely, unpredictable, unfair, and violent. While it's understandable that we want our lives to be something they can't be this side of heaven, the psychological foundation of addiction is laid when we find ways to escape having to feel our true feelings and to deal with life on life's terms.

The psychological catalysts for addiction are three things that come from our lack of skill and practice at remaining healthy through relationship:

1. the demand that life be something it isn't (illusion)
2. the disconnecting of ourselves from our own reality (dissociation)
3. the inability to see or know what is true (denial)

These things are attempts to control our perception or experience of the meaning of our lives. They allow us to temporarily avoid the insecurity of depending on others or God for fulfillment—especially in times of distress, anxiety, loneliness, fatigue, shame, or joy.

Psychological mood altering is akin to looking out the window of our life stories and, not liking what we see or not being able to stomach what we see, painting a scene on the windowpanes of what we wish our lives were like. The problem is that the image we paint always fades and cracks and reality breaks through. We become obsessed with perpetuating the control.

We become committed to living life on our own terms, not on life's terms.

Emotional and Spiritual

As emotional and spiritual creatures, we are created to live fully in relationship with ourselves, others, and God. Our true meaning and our true purpose are found only in relationship. Many of us have been relationally untutored, ignored, wounded, let down, betrayed, or abused in key relationships. Because of this, we live in an emotional conflict. Life is so difficult and unpredictable that we use our brains to hide our hearts instead of using them to express our hearts. Our brains say, "The world is unsafe. You better take care of yourself." Our hearts say, "I crave relationship and love." This conflict leads us in search of ways to manufacture a sense of emotional belonging, security, and safety without having to risk being vulnerable. At the core of addiction are avoidance and a refusal of vulnerability. Addiction is an attempt to find a full life without having to pay the price of living fully.

Based on past experiences, vulnerability means powerlessness and helplessness. Powerlessness and helplessness mean being harmed, being humiliated, being seen as ridiculous or crazy, being ignored or attacked, being rejected or the unwanted focus, being mistaken and shamed, being seen as needy, being taken advantage of, or simply being exposed as human—and being human is considered shameful. We distrust ourselves.

A protective voice inside us says, "If I show you who I really am, tell you what I really think, ask you for what I really need, you may reject me, laugh at me, take advantage of me, or abandon me." We come to expect another wound. This is a reaction or reflex as opposed to an actual choice. In this way, addiction is truly an emotional issue. We distrust others.

Our intolerance of vulnerability extends beyond our relationships with ourselves and others. Addiction is a spiritual issue because it also impacts our relationship with God. In our toxic shame, we can't believe that God loves us, likes us, and desires our good. Also, for many of us we have earnestly prayed to God for relief and comfort and haven't received it. Instead of an authentic and intimate relationship with God, we depend on our own will and thinking. Paul's Letter to the Ephesians illustrates a similar cycle of spiritual isolation and how our self-will and best thinking set us up for detachment from God.

> I tell you this, and insist on it in the Lord, that you must no longer live as the Gentiles do, in the futility of their thinking. They are darkened in their understanding and separated from the life of God because of the ignorance that is in them due to the hardening of their hearts. Having lost all sensitivity, they have given themselves over to sensuality so as to indulge in every kind of impurity, and they are full of greed. (Eph. 4:17–19)

To defend ourselves from the pain of life, we harden our hearts. When we turn away from how we are made to feel and live, we must fill the void. We turn to mood-altering substances and behaviors to numb our feelings. We find inauthentic substitutes for real relationship that help us survive life but enslave us. In the futility of our thinking, we try to find a way to escape life, and addiction is the result. We distrust God.

83

God created us to live fully in relationship. Full life cannot be found without God fully in it. But we are ashamed of our sensitivity and have contempt for our vulnerability. Becoming open again in how we are created, and becoming willing to reach toward the connection we are made to have with ourselves, others, and God, will render us open to the life we are created to live. And to the possibility that our understanding of God is controlled by past experiences rather than the true nature of God—which is love. God created emotional and spiritual beings who are sensitive to and in need of others and him.

NATE'S STORY OF HOPE

Sweaty and thirsty from my newspaper route, I propped my bike against the front of the building and went inside. The neighborhood grocery was air-conditioned, making it one of the only cool places in town. I selected a grape soda from the pop machine and a Baby Ruth from the candy counter, then started wandering the aisles. I was in no hurry to go home.

Delivering papers had become my daily escape, my excuse to leave the house for a few hours every afternoon. The atmosphere at home had changed dramatically after Mom died. She had been my closest confidante and biggest fan. I missed her every day, but there were no photos of her in the house anymore, and I was finding it hard to remember her face. My siblings and I were not allowed to talk about her. We were Christians, so we were not allowed to grieve. We were certainly not allowed to ask about her sudden disappearance, her undisclosed illness, or the mysterious manner of her death.

Dad decided to remarry. The engagement announcement seemed like good news at the time, but things didn't feel the same at home. For now at least I could escape the tension and dawdle in the dimness of the store, spending as much time as I could out of the house. That's when I saw her for the very first time, the voluptuous, half-naked woman winking at me from the magazine rack. I stopped, transfixed, as an unfamiliar sensation coursed through my body and brain. The only boys' magazine I had ever seen was the Boy Scouts' monthly publication, *Boys' Life*, but this was a boys' magazine of an entirely different kind: *Playboy*. I didn't dare touch the magazine—something told me that to do so would be wrong—but I could not tear myself away from the woman on the cover.

I was eleven years old, and this exposure to pornography took me completely by surprise. Nobody had warned me that pornography even existed. I didn't know that every boy eventually sees porn or that every boy instinctively likes porn because it depicts something we are wired by God to want. I had no clue that my personal vulnerability to porn was being amplified by the ungrieved loss of maternal connection and my attendant yearning for comfort. I knew, somehow, that what I was seeing was wrong, but I didn't know why it was wrong. I just felt guilty for having seen her and ashamed of having liked her. At the dinner table that night, I acted like nothing had happened. But after dinner I slipped out of the house and ran back to the store for one more look.

I maintained a stash of soft-core porn throughout my teenage years. This behavior, of course, was not unusual. Even before the advent of the internet, it was common for adolescent boys to collect porn. What made my collecting especially fateful was that it was always completely secret. I was tortured by guilt and made countless private resolutions to stop, even purging my collection several times, but I never dared tell anyone about my growing fascination with porn. I never even hinted to anyone that I was tempted by porn because to do so would have ruined my reputation as a Christian and killed my chances for a career in ministry.

Since I often heard that "it's better to marry than to burn," I assumed that marriage would ultimately solve my lust problem. During my college years, I rationalized my porn use as "preparation for marriage," unaware that the material I was using to medicate my loneliness was poisoning my future marriage. Pornography offers an imaginary connection to a virtual person. Those of us who are riddled with insecurity often find this offer irresistible—but if we accept it, porn immediately begins eroding our ability to form and sustain a real connection with an actual person. Long-term porn use creates an intimacy disorder.

I did eventually fall in love with a real live woman who admired my carefully crafted public persona and agreed to marry me. The early days of our marriage were idyllic, but by the time I enrolled in seminary, the honeymoon was over, a child was on the way, my loneliness had returned, and my porn habit had resurfaced. Then it got worse.

My new low came on a trip to New York City, an outing organized by the seminary. The purpose of the trip was to show us how women are exploited by the sex business. This seemed like an excellent educational opportunity to me. Surely a peek behind the curtain would shatter my illusions about pornography and break its spell. I invited my wife to join me on the trip, and when the tour guide ushered us together into a sticky peep-show booth in Times Square, she was the one who put the quarter in. The lights went out, a projector clattered to life in the darkness, flickering figures appeared on the screen, and my world changed.

I did not understand at the time that this grainy movie was far more potent than the still images in the glossy magazines I had been consuming. Movies, after all, are immersive. They are powerful and convincing simulators of human experience, capable of deceiving that primitive part of our brains that cannot distinguish between actual events and virtual ones. My wife was disgusted by this brief exposure to hard-core porn. I mimicked her reaction, careful to conceal my true level of interest, but a few days later, drawn by a longing I could neither explain nor resist, I found myself sneaking away from home and school in search of a source for this new drug.

In the years that followed, I was very, very careful in my pursuit and use of pornography and was never caught. Still, my marriage and family suffered in ways I did not recognize. As my preoccupation with pornography grew, I drifted away from my wife emotionally and missed priceless opportunities for closeness with my kids. I spent hours every day in a dissociated state, disconnected from others and myself, either drowning in despair over my last fix or maneuvering desperately toward the next one. Then it got worse.

I had never imagined that I would be physically unfaithful to my wife. I love my wife. Also, I had become a pastor, and pastors do not commit adultery. My porn use was dangerous, yes, but I now regarded porn as a defense against infidelity. Then, while driving to a candlelight service one Christmas Eve, I pulled over to offer a ride to a woman who was walking in the rain. I had no idea what she was doing until she was in the car and propositioning me. My response was automatic, as though I had been rehearsing it for years. I reached for my wallet.

This first experience with a prostitute was awful but intense, its riskiness triggering a surge of adrenaline. Later that night, awash in regret, I promised God and myself that I would never do that again. I did not pick up another prostitute right away, but eventually I did. And then I did it again, and again, and again.

The months and years that followed were hellish. I despised my own hypocrisy and was terrified of being seen, but despite countless private confessions to God and at least a thousand vows to stop, I could never quit for more than a few days. Finally, when I could no longer cope with the constant anxiety created by my double life, I quit the ministry and went into business, where I had the great misfortune to succeed. Success brought more money than I had ever made in the ministry, with even less accountability, making it possible for my activity to intensify.

My best estimate is that I spent three hundred thousand dollars on pornography and prostitutes during my years of active addiction. More than the money, however, I regret that I spent my children's childhood, along with decades of my wife's life and my own, trading my birthright, day after day, for a bowl of beans.

The nightmare finally ended when, after catching me downloading porn on the internet and finding a condom I could not explain, my wife sat me down on the edge of our bed and simply said, "I'm done." When I tried to explain and apologize, she stopped me. "I still love you," she said, "but I don't like you. I don't trust you, I don't respect you, and I don't believe you can ever change."

I'm told that four out of every five men who seek help for sexually compulsive behavior do so only after receiving an ultimatum from a wife or a girlfriend. I'm one of the four. My wife gave me the gift of desperation. It was only in a last-ditch effort to salvage my only real friendship that I finally became willing to do the unthinkable and reach out for help.

Today, thanks to my addiction, I have been invited out of soul-killing isolation and into honest, life-giving relationships with other perfectly imperfect human beings. After years of dissociated living, I have been taught to cultivate an inner awareness, an attentiveness to my own ongoing experience in the world around me. I have also been allowed to grieve and have found that the very emotions I was denied when I was young are channels to healing and growth.

Nate Larkin is the founder of the Samson Society and author of *Samson and the Pirate Monks: Calling Men to Authentic Brotherhood*. See https://natelarkin.com and https://samsonsociety.com.

HOW NORMAL
BECOMES ADDICTION

Jeremiah (the Old Testament prophet) paints a picture of how we are made to live and how we too often end up living— what is normal and what is common. Jeremiah speaks to the stark difference between a "blessed" person (normal) and a "cursed" person (common).

This is what the LORD says:

> "Cursed is the one who trusts in man,
>   who draws strength from mere flesh
>   and whose heart turns away from the LORD.
> That person will be like a bush in the wastelands;
>   they will not see prosperity when it comes.
> They will dwell in the parched places of the desert,
>   in a salt land where no one lives.

But blessed is the one who trusts in the LORD,
　　whose confidence is in him.
They will be like a tree planted by the water
　　that sends out its roots by the stream.
It does not fear when heat comes;
　　its leaves are always green.
It has no worries in a year of drought
　　and never fails to bear fruit." (Jer. 17:5–8)

What a great metaphor for the human life. Jeremiah says that if we are rooted in the right place and fed by the right things, then even when adversity and struggle come our way, we will be confident and secure. We will have something to give others because we have been fed. On the contrary, if we live in isolation, we will end up doing whatever it takes to survive.

Normal

When a baby is born, medical professionals do the Apgar, a test to quickly acquire an overall assessment of a newborn's well-being. Apgar is an acronym for appearance (skin color), pulse (heart rate), grimace response (reflexes), activity (muscle tone), and respiration (breathing rate and effort). As much as it's a way to tell if a baby is physically healthy, the Apgar also highlights three essential emotional and spiritual characteristics of what it means to live fully.

- Does the child cry out, expressing the fear of not having security and the need for the comfort of care?

- Does the child reach out to experience the touch of another human, the reflex response of connection?
- Does the child take in food, receiving from others what is necessary for growth?

From our birth until our death, we must continue to practice those three things if we are to live fully.

- cry out: express our feelings, needs, desire, longings, and hopes in response to how we are created and the lives we live
- reach out: live in relational dependency and humility and continue to ask for the respect, support, encouragement, and care we need from others
- take in: receive the good that is offered from others so we can offer it to others in return

These three essential elements mark people as capable of emotional and spiritual vitality and connection. If the three essentials are evident, we can live fully. If they are not, our vitality and connection suffer.

We are created as emotional and spiritual creatures, created to do one thing—live fully. We do so by living fully in relationship with ourselves, others, and God. We are created for relationship. Our deepest physical, psychological, emotional, and spiritual drives are for relationship. Remaining vulnerable to relationship is the basis of living fully.

Normal means being sensitive, expressive, needy, and receptive. It means we have the ability to be vulnerable. It means everyday life can get to us. Living fully means staying available to how we are created. We are meant to grow through our vulnerability because it exposes our design for secure relationship with God, others, and even ourselves. Being normal means that we will experience emotional wounds, learn to contend with those wounds, and grow our capacity to mature through our wounds. We are made to cry out, reach out, and take in—that is, to be vulnerable.

Common

The difficulty of being normal is that the common story we share is that life hurts. All of us have experienced emotional and spiritual wounds. This happens to everyone. There is nothing we can do to stop it. When no one is present whom we trust to help us walk through the pain to find healing and reconnection, we often experience this as abandonment, and we become ashamed of how we are made as feeling and needing creatures. In this loneliness and shame, we respond by making vows to survive. Though often quite simple and often made in silence and in secret, these vows go a long way toward walling off our hearts. Examples of these vows are the following:

- "I won't let that happen again."
- "They can't get to me."
- "I'll never care that much again."
- "I can't let people know what I did or how I feel."
- "I'm going to make sure I'm safe."
- "I will only be loved for what I do for others."

- "I can only be loved if I succeed."
- "I must remain alone to be safe."

The problem is that these vows are difficult to keep because they go against how God created us. So in order to keep these vows, we construct emotional survival strategies to get our needs met without exposing our hearts to vulnerability. We get very creative in our survival strategies, often using the gifts of our intellect (being smart), willpower (trying hard), and morality (being good) to become experts at hiding our hearts. We practice forms of being safe and in control instead of being truthful and present. We find ways to appease, please, caretake, seek approval, and achieve so we can be valued. Our effort and our performance take the place of the presence of our true Selves.

This performance is emotionally and spiritually exhausting. We become isolated as a way of staying safe. We become survivors. The more emotionally isolated we become, the more self-centered we become. In an effort to protect our hearts, we hide them from ourselves and others.

One unique thing about humans is our ability to deny how we are made. No other creature can do this. Every living thing is reaching to experience its fullness, its completion—its own living fully. This reality is true of trees, horses, and humans. However, humans have the ability, through our amazing intellect, to hide the reality of how we are created. We have the power, creativity, and ingenuity to attempt to avoid the vulnerable expression of life's desire within us. To state again for emphasis: we often use God's gifts of intellect, willpower, and morality to hide what is in our hearts in order to avoid the pain of being imperfect, needy creatures who need relationship to thrive.

Sadly, many of us aren't raised in homes or in cultures where we are helped to express our hearts. We fear and distrust ourselves with others. We subtly (or not so subtly) deny or block efforts at relationship—and ultimately love—instead of being open. Closing ourselves off and isolating ourselves are understandable. However, our very real reasons and justifications for doing so do not change how we are created.

Unfortunately, in small and large ways, we are often emotionally, physically, or spiritually abandoned by those we love the most. Sometimes we are trained (or we train ourselves) to reject, deaden, or hide our hearts. And sometimes the only choice we have is to hide our hearts from ourselves and others in order to protect our true Selves. Consequently, we don't know how to use our feelings, needs, desire, longings, and hopes to live fully. We don't know how to handle those things that have wounded us. We become defensive, survival oriented, withdrawn, numb, and self-sufficient.

Instead of expressing our hearts, we hide our hearts and attempt to bury our roots. In other words, we run from clumsiness. We run from being known. We run from having to be vulnerable to experience love and life and to give ourselves to someone else—because when we do, we can get hurt. Our tragedy is that we invest in the common (self-protection) and avoid the normal (the ability to be vulnerable).

When the roots of our hearts aren't fed the emotional and spiritual food of relational intimacy with ourselves, others, and God, our hearts do not thrive. They only survive. As damaging as this strategy of self-protection is to ourselves and to those who need us the most, it becomes the "best choice" we have until we become willing to change.

All of us have experienced relational wounds and are relationally impaired. One reason is because the people who were raising us (or the culture that was raising us) had their own impaired attachment styles of relating. We didn't get the affirmation or the confirmation we needed because our caregivers didn't give it to us because they had shut down part of their hearts. To the degree that our parents, caregivers, and culture were emotionally, spiritually, or psychologically impaired, we will grow up impaired.

The other reason we have impaired styles of relating is because we experienced some kind of emotional or physical trauma growing up. When we experience trauma, we become emotionally and psychologically confused and overwhelmed to the extent that we can't make sense of what happened. Trauma isn't just the obvious things such as sexual abuse, physical abuse, the sudden death of a loved one, divorce, or a tragic illness or injury. These "Big T" traumas are significant, but there are also more subtle "little t" traumas. These are often the common ways we have been mistreated (especially when we were children). Some examples are when parents, teachers, coaches, mentors, or other authority figures do the following:

- play mind games with a child
- rage at a child
- withdraw from or abandon a child (like when a parent is in a severe depression, addiction, or illness)
- are consistently passive-aggressive or sarcastic with a child

- have erratic mood swings and are emotionally unpredictable
- are one way at home and another way in public

When our wounds come from our parents, caregivers, and mentors, they are very damaging. This is true not only for children but also for adults. When our relationships with spouses, parents, friends, coworkers, siblings, or neighbors have these elements, they are also damaging. This is especially true with authority figures. When we are adults and people who have authority in our lives (spiritual leaders, employers, mentors, etc.) abandon, betray, or take advantage of us, the situation can be particularly traumatic. (And even when authority figures don't do these things, it can feel as though they are if we have experienced such things in childhood. We misinterpret the words and actions of authority because we see them through the eyes of past experiences. We don't know what is best for us, and we put our trust in others who may not know what is best for us either.)

Whether we experience these kinds of relationships as a child or an adult, they create a swirl of ambivalence in our hearts. When the people we need to go to for help to make sense of life's tragedies are not able to be present with us in our pain, fear, and shame, we are left emotionally and spiritually alone. When they use us for their own personal advantage, the emotional abandonment and trauma interfere with (or, if the combination is bad enough, even shatter) our connection to ourselves, to others, and to God. When this happens, we feel worthless and live in a cloud of toxic shame. We say things to ourselves like "What's wrong with me?" "I must be too much." "I'm too needy."

In toxic shame, we don't trust how God made us. We reject and rebel against how we are made. The contempt we have for ourselves as emotional and relational people leads us to try to earn our worth through performance, people pleasing, achieving, and caretaking. Our identity is shaped by the affirmation of our performance. We end up feeling loved only for our success—especially if the success brings the temporary affirmation of others. We end up trying to earn the love of others through being good and doing good. Running from what is normal is common, and it is what leads us to addiction.

Addiction Is a Cycle of Survival

Addiction has many homes. There are obvious ones in dark alleys and deeply covert ones in the living rooms of suburban houses and the pews of churches. No matter the home, though, addiction is an enslavement that occurs when we attempt to escape life because how we are made renders us needy. Addiction temporarily works to stop the struggle of neediness and vulnerability. For a moment, we get to have a sense of security, confidence, safety, and peace without having to experience and express the vulnerability of feelings and needs. In other words, we find a way to manufacture a sense of well-being without the difficulties of relationship, the risk of rejection, the heartbreak of betrayal, the stress of perseverance, or the struggle of resiliency. Addiction is an impaired attempt to live fully without having to pay the price of feeling fully.

One great tragedy of addiction is that, to our brains, it often seems like the real thing or sometimes even better than the real thing. Addiction operates as a tragic emotional and spiritual counterfeit substitute for living connected to one's self, others, and God. Addiction is built by the repetitive use of substances and behaviors that soothe, comfort, exhilarate, calm, excite, stimulate, focus, and even mimic intimacy with others and God.

Addicts, of any sort, don't believe, trust, or know that our emotional experience of life is a gift. We distrust and abhor feelings of sadness, hurt, anger, loneliness, fear, shame, guilt, and gladness. We feel threatened by our need for belonging, mattering, touch, grief, attention, guidance, and support. We cannot accept our feelings and needs as God-given tools that allow us to live fully, love deeply, and even lead well a life in a tragic place. In this way, at its core, addiction is an emotional and spiritual issue more than a physical illness and a psychological compulsion. Our craving for relational connection is so powerful that we will find it legitimately or illegitimately.

As we develop contempt for and become ashamed of how we are created, we become intolerant of vulnerability. When this happens, our interactions with others, God, and even ourselves become centered around avoiding the experience of the inner Self—the feelings, needs, desire, longings, and hopes that are inherent in the heart of every one of us. Instead of living fully, we live lives that revolve around a spiraling cycle of survival that becomes addiction. In the survival cycle of addiction, our minds go dull, our bodies grow tired, and our hearts go numb—but we still want to feel alive. To create that sense of aliveness, we do something or take something to create the physical, psychological, emotional, or spiritual experience we *want* instead of the experience we *have*. Here is how it plays out.

The Addiction Cycle

Life Events

Our days are filled with events, and for every event, we have feelings, thoughts, and needs. That is the nature and reality of life. Whenever an event is difficult, stressful, potentially shameful, or painful, we have feelings, thoughts, and needs for which we want help and relief. Life events render us vulnerable to physical, psychological, emotional, and spiritual pain, stress, uncertainty, and fatigue. Our reaction to avoiding vulnerability triggers anxiety.

Anxiety

Anxiety puts us on high alert, on the lookout for an anticipated danger (often imaginary). Anxiety very often relates to the fear of reexperiencing events of the past that rendered us helpless, hurt, in need, or ashamed. Anxiety often triggers thoughts and actions that are attempts to prevent humiliation, embarrassment, toxic shame, or helplessness. Physically, anxiety is the brain's freeze, fight, flight response. Psychologically, it is the imagining of negative outcomes. Emotionally, it is the anticipation of something happening that we believe will make us helpless. Spiritually, it is the fear of God's lack of presence, goodness, or care.

While humans are exceptionally good at feeling and at connecting our feelings to memories, we are not so good at connecting our feelings and memories to thoughts. The parts of the brain that feel and remember are not the same parts of the brain that think. Anxiety that isn't processed and connected to an internal awareness of where it is coming from and what we fear becomes a toxic experience.

Control

In our anxiety, we begin to seek ways (often unconsciously) to control our environment, circumstances, and relationships so that we can return to feeling safe, secure, and confident. Instead of knowing how to identify, explore, and express our feelings in relationships, we take actions to ward off anxiety. We begin to read the minds of others—we think we know what they are feeling, needing, and thinking. We anticipate what they are going to do next. We make up stories about things that need to be prevented and project our anxiety onto others. We become preoccupied with controlling our environment, circumstances, and relationships so that we no longer feel vulnerable to life and can stay in control.

Preoccupation

Over time, as our anxiety becomes second nature, we become hypervigilant, always on guard, always looking out for the next event that could catch us unaware. We overinterpret our world from the context of threats of rejection, loss, or humiliation. In the preoccupation phase of the addiction cycle, we take responsibility for others' feelings, thoughts, moods, and actions. We have to anticipate what others are feeling and thinking so that our anxious fantasies will not be fulfilled. We preoccupy ourselves with whatever we need to feel better.

Relief Seeking

Though they quell anxiety temporarily, watchfulness and carefulness are exhausting. About the time we get close to having a sense that our anxiety, control, and preoccupation might deliver us from the "threatening event" we anticipate, we begin to recognize how internally tired we are. Relief seeking is the need for the reward for all the "hard work" of surviving life. Finding a way to fix our internal world becomes the goal. We start looking for something to do or something to take to save us from and cure us of our hypervigilance, dread, anxiety, and control. We have to get a break from the stresses that life is putting on us and the pressure we are putting on ourselves.

Self-Cure

When we do or take "it," we are temporarily satiated. "It" can be sugar, alcohol, exercise, video games, pornography, shopping, work, worry, drugs, cutting, and so on. Regardless of the "it" we use for relief, we have something that gives us a break from ourselves for a little while. Whatever the "it," our self-cure drug-of-choice use grows more frequent and more severe, and as it does, so do the negative consequences. One drink eventually becomes four, and four become six. One dose of nicotine becomes a pack. The initial fun of social media becomes an obsession. A quick text or email ends up as an argument at dinner. Exercise takes the place of significant family events. The new television series becomes an all-night media binge leading to being late for work or school the next day.

Despair

When the relief ends, we feel regret. "I wish I hadn't done that." As the frequency, severity, and consequences of our actions begin to intensify, we experience a growing sense of despair. We begin to recognize the trouble around us. We may recognize that we missed a birthday party or forgot a work responsibility, or we may simply have a sense of being in trouble—with ourselves, others, or God. We experience regret and remorse and, along with them, self-contempt and self-condemnation.

Promises, Plans, and Willpower

Because of our despair, we know we need to change. Instead of asking for the help we need, we make promises to stop and swear we will change. We formulate plans to make us well. We start working to make up for our shame and others' wounded feelings and suspicions. But the promises and the plans "not to do that again" are really attempts not to do that again in the same way. We do all this alone.

In shame, we isolate ourselves. Our self-cure has replaced genuine relationship.

The promises we make, the plans that follow, and the effort we apply are always an external solution to an internal problem of the heart. To deepen the tragedy, the only tool we have to enact the promises and the plans is the power of our own will. We don't know how to receive help, and we will not permit ourselves to be helped where the help is most needed. We are going to be our own solution. Our self-blame means having to self-will the fix. We caused the problem, we believe, and therefore we must fix it. We cannot face that we are enslaved to the self-cure. And if we do know it, we don't dare allow anyone else to get control of us. The problem with making promises and plans and using willpower is that these efforts work on addiction like they work on diarrhea—they don't.

Repetition

While we are working on our plans to keep our promises, life goes on. New events happen, about which we have feelings that we don't recognize and don't know what to do with. We face vulnerability again. Guaranteed. Life doesn't change, and the cycle of survival begins again.

The cycle will slowly or quickly become a downward spiral, its centripetal force increasing with every episode and negative consequence. As the cycle tightens, the self-cure becomes the center of our world. We experience the centripetal force that draws us closer and closer to the dragon's belly as well as to those who are in denial with us. All others are flung further and further away from the person they love or wish good for.

Once we've done this cycle a few times, we begin to wear a path. With more repetition, the path starts to get some ruts in it. In not too long a time, the ruts grow so deep that they become tracks that are far easier to follow than not. We become trapped in a cycle of survival following the tracks of addiction. A train goes where the tracks are laid, no matter what a passenger has planned otherwise.

While this cycle will harm us and ultimately destroy us, it also paradoxically comforts us. The addiction cycle temporarily relieves us of the pain and anxiety of being human. Addiction is so powerful because it works.

Survival requires doing whatever is needed to block the emotional pains of the past from being repeated. The great tragedy is that the future can never become different from the past. In survival, all of our movements are about the past and preventing recurrence. And since we are in denial, we don't even realize that we are in a repetitive cycle. It is a long, slow train right back to the same depot where it started. We condition ourselves to stay on guard waiting for the next terrible event.

SARAH'S STORY OF HOPE

It was a warm summer afternoon, and the sun was streaming through my bedroom window. I woke up from a nap and had this resounding sense of peace. I thought, *My life is perfect! My performance has paid off! I have a husband in full-time ministry, a nursing job I love, and a cute house in a transitional neighborhood.*

I loved to compare my life to the lives of others and feel pride over how I "got it right." I also loved to fix other people. I became the go-to Christian girl for advice and solutions.

All of that was before "life happened" to me.

I began a long and painful journey of infertility, which led my husband and me to consider adoption. Our hopeful start to a family was shattered by a failed adoption. I began to wonder what I was doing wrong. I had followed all the "rules" of being a good Christian. I had grown up in a home where I had been taught that performance was the key to fixing life. Walking on eggshells and spinning plates were my greatest talents. I could hear the slight crack of an eggshell in plenty of time to prevent the shatter. I had learned to become small and hide my heart. I could read the faces of others to determine how fast or slow to spin the plates to get their approval, but the pain of infertility and the journey of a failed adoption cut into my performance.

My perfect life was falling apart, and I could not fix it. Rather than feeling my pain and grieving my loss, I got busy—busy making sure everyone else was okay.

I was really good at denial. I looked the other way at my husband's addiction to pornography. I looked the other way at his rage. I kept secrets about how I struggled in relationship with my husband. I began to live in fantasy about how my life would be so much better if only _____ were different. My husband became my enemy. I spent hours resenting him. I talked myself out of feeling hurt, lonely, or angry. I talked myself out of feeling anything. The talents of my childhood returned with a resounding encore. I worked tirelessly to stay small, say only what others wanted to hear, and constantly read faces. I would be okay if I could just make everyone else okay.

The sunshine of life peeked through my window when we adopted a precious baby a few years later and miraculously became pregnant a few months later. I became a mom of two beautiful children within a short time. I loved being a mom, and I loved working hard at being the perfect mom. I read books on parenting about how to discipline, schedule, and grow godly children. I would not let my husband help much with the children for fear he would not "get it right." Then I resented him for not being more involved. I left him in an impossible position and hated him for not rescuing me.

Self-sufficiency became a new goal. In a short amount of time, the areas of my life that had not been wrecked by marriage became wrecked by motherhood. Our adopted child was diagnosed with autism. I had never felt more afraid, alone, and out of control. The eggshells surrounding me were beginning to crack, and the plates were starting to fall. The noise was deafening. I felt like I was going to die. The finale to my performance began the day my husband disclosed he was having an affair.

Everything shattered. I was at the end of myself.

Sitting in the office of our marriage therapist, my husband told me he was in love with another woman. She was the escape, the way out of the pain of our marriage. Waves of nausea crashed over me, the air seemed to leave the room, and I remember grabbing the garbage can, thinking I was about to vomit. I tried to breathe in between the deep sobs of my pain. A gracious friend picked me up and drove me home. My husband and I made a plan for him to move his things out of our home and live in an apartment. We made a schedule for him to visit our children, as we would now coparent.

After the shock of his affair began to lift, deep down inside me a spark of hope began to grow. A voice that I had quieted for many, many years began to tell the truth. I began to allow myself to feel the pain of my life, grieve deeply, and trust God with my story. I had read the book *The Voice of the Heart* and began to name my feelings. I started calling safe friends to talk about what was going on inside of me. I began to tell the truth. It felt so good to let go of my secrets and have someone else say, "I know what that is like. I am so sorry." This was not the life I had dreamed of. My fairy-tale story was wrecked, but something was awakening inside of me. I still had hope.

A few months later, my husband went to residential treatment for ninety days for sex addiction. I began to understand my part in the unraveling of our relationship. My codependency played a huge role in keeping us both sick. I slowly stopped focusing on my husband being the problem and started looking at myself.

My inability to tell the truth of my heart, my ability to manipulate others to get my needs met, and allowing someone else to determine my truth were all ways that I had kept the eggshells intact and the plates spinning.

Through working the 12-step program of recovery in S-Anon (a world-wide fellowship of the relatives and friends of sexually addicted people) and continuing individual counseling, I began to find my voice. I began to believe that I was worthy of love, and the toxic, shame-filled messages of "You are not enough" began to quiet.

My husband began his own journey of recovery, and through lots of willingness, patience, time, and work, we slowly started rebuilding our marriage. Our journey has been wrought with many valleys and peaks.

Living life with a child with autism has required me to learn much about the meaning of self-care. Going to meetings, working my steps, and living in authentic relationship have become vital parts of accepting life the way God is writing my story.

Some days I slip right back into my codependency, thinking and demanding that others must be okay for me to be okay. But I am grateful for my relationships in recovery. I can call for help. I have women who can hear my truth and give me their experience, strength, and hope. I can see my disease, reframe my thinking, and live out a life of surrender and acceptance. I am grateful for my recovery.

6

AM I ADDICTED?

It's easy to view addiction as someone else's problem. The reality is that addiction is pervasive, personal, cultural, and even institutional. It's everywhere. It's the most dominant influence in the culture of America—in secular and religious cultures, urban and rural settings, professional and blue-collar worlds. Because addiction has so many faces, is fueled by denial, and can look so acceptable (even laudable), it's wiser to ask, "*Where* is addiction in my life?" than to ask, "*Is* addiction in my life?"

A massive number of people in the world are drifting toward or are trapped in addiction. Many more of us than we are comfortable admitting are in some form of relationally and physically damaging addiction. Too often the consequences just haven't caught up with us yet. Addiction has not disrupted our status quo enough to break our denial. Although being honest with ourselves can be painful, the road to full living and freedom begins here.

Every natural instinct cries out against the idea of personal powerlessness.

Because addiction is fueled by denial, just because we don't see it doesn't mean we're not enslaved by it. By going back in our own stories, and with perspective and clarity and courage, we can begin to see that for years before we realized it, our lives were out of control, that our addiction was indeed the beginning of a fatal progression. With addiction, we most often don't see how infested and overgrown our lives are by it until we begin to find freedom from it. But once we look, we often begin to see the ways we are entangled and captive. We start to see that all the things we thought were good are not so good. We start to see that our best efforts are getting us nowhere and our good intentions are not so good. The apostle Paul said it so clearly about himself in his letter to fellow Christians in Rome.

> I do not understand what I do. For what I want to do, I do not do, but what I hate I do. And if I do what I do not want to do, I agree that the law is good. As it is, it is no longer I myself who do it, but it is sin living in me. For I know that good itself does not dwell in me, that is, in my sinful nature. For I have the desire to do what is good, but I cannot carry it out. For I do not do the good I want to do, but the evil I do not want to do—this I keep on doing. Now if I do what I do not want to do, it is no longer I who do it, but it is sin living in me that does it. (Rom. 7:15–20)

Beginning to see and admit to ourselves where we *really* are and what we *really* are doing is the first step toward freedom. Being honest with ourselves, like Paul, about our powerlessness and unmanageability requires that we become willing to put aside pride.

A Thorough Self-Examination

No one can tell anyone else that they are an addict. Each person has to be willing to admit this for themselves.

The following questions provide an opportunity for you to be honest with yourself and with God. These questions will help you see if the thoughts, behaviors, and reactions in your life support an addiction. Your willingness to be honest in answering these questions can blow away the fog of denial if it is there.

The purpose of this exercise is not for you to judge where you have been right or wrong. The purpose is for you to admit to yourself where you are powerless, where your life is unmanageable by your thinking and efforts alone—where attempts to be happy have led you to become enslaved.

You don't have to answer every question. You may not connect with every question. But please be conscientious and let yourself find plenty of examples where appropriate. Give yourself time to think about your answers, recall pertinent memories, and make notes on your discoveries. An exercise like this doesn't have to be well written, but make sure your notes are clear so that you can understand them later. Record your responses in a notebook, journal, or whatever device you're most comfortable with (phone, laptop, etc.).

You don't have to show your answers to anyone. They are to help you understand your personal experience and maybe open the eyes of your heart a bit wider and make your vision a bit clearer.

Before you begin, take a moment to pray specifically for clarity, willingness, openness, and honesty.

Now proceed with the exercise, which comprises three parts. First, explain how you do and do not identify with these five statements:

1. I regularly feel uneasy or anxious.
2. I try to impress people or make people think highly of me.
3. I genuinely like myself and enjoy being me.
4. If someone saw the real me, I would want to run away and hide.
5. I have trouble going to sleep or sleeping through the night, and I believe the root cause is emotional, psychological, or spiritual.

Second, the following table lists common substances and behaviors that can be addictive. Three statements correspond with each item. In the space provided, put a mark by each item and corresponding statement that is true for you.

After reviewing the inventory, what do you notice? What new insights and awareness do you have about yourself?

Third, choose one item from the list of substances and behaviors in the table and answer the questions that follow. If you have trouble picking an item, choose the one you would be the least willing to go without.

Common Addictive SUBSTANCES and BEHAVIORS	I use or have used this to feel better or different or to fit in.	I do not want others to know about this.	I am not willing to go without this or to recognize that I would have trouble going without it.
Alcohol			
Pornography			
Romance/Dating			
Prescription/ Over the Counter Medications (*using when not prescribed or using more than prescribed*)			
Elicit/Illegal Drugs			
Cannabis			
Tobacco/Nicotine			
Food (*binge eating, not eating, or yo-yo dieting*)			
Sex (*either inside or outside of marriage*)			
Computers/Internet			
Social Media			
Video Games			
Digital Media/ Television			
Working/ Volunteering			
Caffeine (*coffee, soda, etc.*)			
Exercise			

Common Addictive SUBSTANCES and BEHAVIORS	I use or have used this to feel better or different or to fit in.	I do not want others to know about this.	I am not willing to go without this or to recognize that I would have trouble going without it.
Achievement			
Spiritual Obsession (as opposed to religious devotion)			
Pain (seeking)			
Cutting			
Shopping			
Sleep			
Plastic Surgery			
Codependence/ People Pleasing			
Rage			
Sports (high school, college, or professional)			
Other			
Other			
Other			

Initial Experiences with This Substance or Behavior

1. Describe the first time you experienced this substance or behavior.

2. When you initially experienced this substance or behavior, how did it make you feel?

How This Substance or Behavior Affects You Mentally

1. Have you had a pattern of not remembering what you just did? If so, please describe.
2. Have you obsessed about using this substance or engaging in this behavior? If so, please describe.
3. Have you ever felt like you were going to go insane or lose your mind? If so, please describe.
4. Have you lied to yourself (distorted the facts) about what really happened or what you have really done? If so, please describe.

How This Substance or Behavior Affects You Relationally

1. How has this substance or behavior affected your relationships?
2. How has this substance or behavior hurt others in your life (spouse, children, family, friends, and colleagues)?
3. Have you gotten into a relationship with someone you would not normally associate with because of this substance or behavior?
4. When have you been dishonest with others regarding this substance or behavior? How did you lie?
5. Have you misled others or yourself by omitting facts about your use of this substance or behavior? If so, please describe.
6. Have you led a secret life? If so, please describe.
7. How have you pretended not to be affected by your use of this substance or behavior, and what was that like?

How This Substance or Behavior Affects You Spiritually

1. How has this substance or behavior affected you spiritually?
2. How has this substance or behavior affected your relationship with God?
3. What are the spiritual consequences of using this substance or engaging in this behavior?
4. Has this substance or behavior led you to ignore your morals, values, or philosophy of living?

How This Substance or Behavior Affects You Emotionally

1. How has this substance or behavior affected you emotionally?
2. Have you been anxious or depressed? If so, please describe.
3. Have you tried to control your emotions by using this substance or engaging in this behavior? Did it work?
4. How has this substance or behavior numbed your shame or anxiety?
5. Have you experienced any long-term emotional effects of your use of this substance or behavior? If so, please describe.
6. Have you felt guilty because of using this substance or doing this behavior? If so, please describe.
7. Are you often grumpy, irritable, and resentful? If so, please describe.

8. Have you felt shameful about yourself because of your use of this substance or behavior? If so, please describe.

How This Substance or Behavior Affects You Physically

1. How has this substance or behavior affected you physically?
2. Have you hurt yourself while using this substance or engaging in this behavior? If so, please describe.
3. Have you neglected or harmed your body because of this substance or behavior (e.g., missed sleep, overslept, gotten injured, developed a chronic medical condition)? If so, please describe.
4. Have you minimized the effects this substance or behavior has had on your body? If so, please describe.
5. Have there been any dangerous episodes related to this substance or behavior? If so, please describe.

How This Substance or Behavior Affects You Financially

1. How has this substance or behavior affected you financially?
2. How much money have you mismanaged or lost because of this substance or behavior?
3. How much money have you spent on this substance or behavior (estimate)?

Attempts to Stop Using This Substance or Engaging in This Behavior

1. Have you used anniversaries, birthdays, special days, or seasons to try to stop using this substance or engaging in this behavior? If so, please describe.
2. Have you made promises to yourself and others that you would stop and then did it again? If so, please describe.
3. In what ways have you tried to stop that didn't work? Examples:
   - tried to stop drinking by having just one drink
   - tried to stop lusting by getting rid of the internet
   - tried to stop spending by being on a strict budget
   - tried to stop overeating by being on a diet
4. What would it be like for you to abstain from this substance or behavior for thirty days? Would it be possible?
5. How willing are you to abstain for thirty days?

Reflection and Summation

Now that you have answered these questions and looked honestly at your relationship with a specific substance or behavior, what new awareness or insights do you have?

Please review your answers and write a summary of what you discovered about yourself.

TODD'S STORY OF HOPE

The image of my house as I strolled down the street with my wife while walking the dog brought up a myriad of feelings. Just weeks before in preparation for an upcoming party, I had decided to steal medications from the pharmacy I was managing with the thought I would never get caught. During this evening walk, I knew my ability to manipulate this outcome was going to be low, but I thought there was no way God was going to take away my home. My wife and daughter had no idea of the turmoil that was going on inside me, and I was grappling with an ego that continued to tell me, "There is no way you will get caught. Just keep lying. You are in control."

As I was growing up, my home life was rich with working parents who fostered a supportive environment and a love that was always present. Neither of my parents was college educated, but the expectation was that my brother and I would go to school and do well as a way to open up opportunities they had never been afforded. My mom and dad were always in motion trying to support our middle-class life, and a healthy work ethic was always present. This was something I would grapple with later in life.

God was someone I was exposed to at an early age, and I remember going to Sunday school and church. We didn't go as a family, but my brother and I would go. My dad would be at work, and Mom would be cleaning the house and getting ready for Sunday lunch. I found peace there but could never figure it out. However, I always reflected on moments in that church and the peace that would envelop me.

From my early years, I never felt like I belonged. I was intensely emotional and, in many situations, would cry if something didn't go my way—if I didn't make the team, if I didn't know the answer to a question, if I thought someone was making fun of me. The feelings, which I now can describe as fear, were crippling. However, I thrived academically and athletically, which I now know I used to adapt and build relationships.

121

I remember my first drink. I was in fourth grade, and it was just a sip of beer while riding with my dad and his friend after a long day of work. His friend was a jack-of-all-trades, and I thought he was the coolest guy ever. Later in life, I would judge him and act as if I didn't know him because I was embarrassed by his actions. At this point, though, I knew him as an interesting guy who hung out with Dad all the time.

After a long day, their routine was to stop at the local gas station to get a six-pack of beer. Each would drink three, but I was allowed to hold the beer as we drove around my small town. My first taste of beer was just a sip, but the taste and feeling of that first beer stuck with me for decades. What stayed with me wasn't just the taste; it was the entire environment: the truck, two of my favorite guys at that age, and riding around with the windows down. It was an awesome feeling.

Moments of perceived freedom came with that first drink. I didn't drink to celebrate. I drank to fit in, and I drank to avoid feeling sad. In high school, weekend drinking was routine. Asking someone from the local store to buy a twenty-four pack of beer for me was common. I liked the feeling of having a few beers with me. The weekends turned into a few days a week in college, and I thought nothing about the time and money I spent on drinking or the gradual apathetic approach I took to school. My desire to go to college was motivated by my self-loathing. I never wanted to move back to my small town, and school was my out. At some point, every night out became consuming enough drinks to get me drunk. This usually led to missing classes and even resulted in a few minor run-ins with local police. However, I made it through college and landed in a professional program that filled me with pride.

The spring before starting my professional program, I was looking for the next high. Alcohol was fun and I had partaken of pot, but I was drawn to the allure of cocaine. It had been around me throughout undergraduate studies, but I had always stuck to alcohol. However, one specific night, I decided to try a little. It is hard to describe the feeling. It was utopia. My inadequacies melted away. My heart raced. I was full of confidence, and the blend of alcohol and this stimulant made me feel like I could do anything. I had found the new concoction that I would pursue throughout my third decade of life.

I partied. Went to class. Did well in school. Worked hard. Got opportunities and used my ability to use people to get what I wanted. This worked for a long time, and I had many great professional opportunities. Upon completion of my professional degree, I felt incomplete. Call it scared of the real world, motivated for more, seeking the ego boost of more education, or looking for another world in which to allow my alcohol and drug use to escalate. I enrolled in another two-year graduate program that sought to build leaders in the world of my professional life.

It was awesome. I lived in a larger city, and no one knew me as the guy from a small town. No one knew me as having parents who weren't educated or lived paycheck to paycheck (the majority of which they were sending to me). I was in a safe zone to work hard and party hard. People within the program had that same approach, and I slowly allowed this world to consume everything about me. There was only professional development. No personal development. No exercise. No spiritual outlet. I even doubted the existence of God—it just simply wasn't possible. I controlled my outcomes, and I could work, study, and outmaneuver to get what I wanted.

Throughout this adventure of higher education, I was dating someone who could qualify as my girlfriend. We were together more than separate, but my loyalty was always in question depending on the situation and where my addiction took me. The times I did not value this relationship provided some of the lowest points of my addiction. I couldn't figure out why I couldn't be content, and in the haze of alcohol and cocaine, I consumed life and those around me. This woman was with me throughout this time, but it was a lifestyle she was willing to walk away from.

The guilt and shame provided some nadir moments. As our relationship continued, I knew inside that I loved her deeply, but when the voice of my addiction took over, I had zero inhibitions. I was like a yo-yo every week. Still,

I managed to get a great first job, and my girlfriend became my wife. After graduating, I knew I was mature and that life out of the educational bubble would become normal.

Around this time, my mom began experiencing health issues. I was hours away and would hear about her struggles to find healthcare. I looked at her as a burden with all of her questions, and I thought if she could just get the right doctor, she would be fine. What I didn't see was that an undiagnosed disease was slowly devouring this strong woman. It worked from the inside out, and until it was finally diagnosed, I made her feel guilty for wasting my time with her questions.

The diagnosis came, she started medication, and my wife became pregnant with our first child. I had arrived. However, every week I was drinking from Thursday evening to Sunday night. I loved staying at home and would only go out with people when I had access to drugs. I loved the cycle and continued on a path of destruction when it came to my relationship with my wife. In fact, at one point, I couldn't have cared less about my new family and thought that life was all about letting my will drive everything and anything.

Going back home to my small town, although I always wanted to leave again, felt good for brief times. Summer trips, weddings, and occasional visits were fun during this period. In fact, I always looked forward to going home for Christmas. I didn't care about the meaning of the holiday, but my conscience seemed to find rest there. In my small town, my drinking was heavy but not as bad. My drug use was minimal because drugs were hard to find. And I could feel like I felt in my younger days. I felt safe.

I thought one Christmas was going to be one of those great trips. Mom was taking medication and feeling better. I was so ready to show everyone I had arrived. We got to my parents' house, and Mom clearly wasn't feeling well. The medication she was taking was resolving the disorder, but it was making her susceptible to infection. In addition, the disorder had gradually made her heart and kidneys decline. So when I arrived and she was bedridden, I didn't know what to do.

How dare she get sick like this for the holidays! Can't she suck it up? said my inner voice. I scoffed at her sickness but had a few drinks and heard how bad she had been feeling (she would never tell me that over the phone). After a family get-together on Christmas Eve, I decided to walk over to check on her. She was sitting in a chair in our living room. She was asleep. I watched. Her breathing was slow, but she looked at peace. I left and came back to the house an hour later. She was crumpled on the floor of the bathroom. I thought she had fallen, but she was too weak to get back to the chair.

I knew Mom needed to go to the emergency room. I scooped her up. She had lost thirty to forty pounds over the year. I remember her being so light. Her bones pressed against my skin, and I remember trying to speak confidence in her. When we got to the hospital, she received some fluids and came around quickly. I thought that was it. Just dehydrated. I remember holding her hand. I can still feel her hand today. It was so thin. She looked up at me and said, "I love you."

I told her, "You scared me. I don't want you to leave us yet."

She responded with a warm gaze. "I am not ready yet either."

After a few hours, some antibiotics, and more fluids, I thought it was safe to go home to get stuff ready for Christmas Day. Mom wanted me to go home and take care of my baby. So I left around 9 p.m.

I went home and jumped in the shower. I was thinking about everything—life, jobs, hope for better health, the feeling of no control—and then the phone rang. It was Dad.

"You need to come back. Something is wrong. They asked me to leave your mom's room, and I can see through the cracked door of the ICU that there are people in her room. What do you think that means?"

"I'm not sure, Dad. I'm sure they are taking care of her." She had been talking to me an hour earlier, but my gut told me something was wrong.

When I arrived at this small community hospital, there wasn't much going on, but there was a lot of activity in the ICU. I can still see my mom's body in the room. The light over her. The nurse feverishly trying to pump air into her lungs.

I thought, *How did we get here? What in the world happened?* It was a pivotal moment I would play in my head for the next three years of my life. I would use this moment to fuel my addiction. My mom's death was not something I knew how to grieve.

About a year later, I accepted a job closer to home. By this point, I drank every day. I was a functional drunk with only minor physical ailments. However, my hangovers were becoming harder to get over. At some point with the move and new job, I decided to divert drugs from my employer. It was a conscious decision that was intended to allow me to party more. I had no concern for the fact that I was jeopardizing my career and my family.

One day I was notified that the drugs I had taken from the automated controlled system had created a discrepancy. I tried to fix it, lie, manipulate, and blame other people. This time it was over. I had to choose to continue to lie and face jail time or tell the truth and ask for help.

It was a divine moment. I asked for help. The people in the room that day gracefully allowed me to get help. For the next four months, I was away from my wife and child and exposed to the meanings of a word I now know as hope.

I was happy to be rid of alcohol and drugs. However, I found myself struggling with feelings I hadn't experienced for over fifteen years. Moments of shame, guilt, loneliness, and sadness were routine. However, strong men in my life began to show me the path through the badlands. The badlands were the beginning of my recovery.

My first few years of staying sober included required 12-step meetings and counseling. I managed to stay sober, but in the third year of my sobriety, I still felt off. Some people in the program talked about the need to develop a connection with a higher power. I didn't know where to start, but my conscience continued to remind me of my time in church when I was young. I also had a good neighbor who was living his life in Christ. I had no idea what this meant, but he had asked me for years to join a men's Bible study. I had always declined, but this time my conscience told me I had to join him.

The first few weekly sessions of the Bible study were uncomfortable. Many of the men were well versed in the Bible. I didn't know the difference between the Old and New Testaments. I found myself routinely wanting to skip. Year one we started with Acts. It was perfect. I could see myself in Paul. I felt relief at reading about his journey, which was all about Jesus, a man I had questioned, scoffed at, and even denied existed.

The second year we studied Romans, and my journey continued. I wanted to live my life as a Christian. Then it happened. Each Monday night after an hour of small group, we would gather in the main sanctuary with the rest of the three hundred men for a review by the study leader. Occasionally, as he prayed to close the session, he would ask if anyone wanted to turn their life over to Christ. I had heard that question for many Mondays the past two and a half years, but something was different that day. The message was sound, and I wanted the guilt of my past to leave me. I wanted to commit my life to Christ.

"If there is anyone here who has heard the message and wants to identify with Christ, simply raise your hand." Each time he prayed that prayer, he would validate those who raised their hands with a simple "Brother, I see your hand." On this night, my heart raced, I began to sweat, and my conscience told me it was time. Jesus was speaking to me: "Raise your hand. I am here." I did it. I raised my hand. "I see you, brother. I see your hand."

I remember thinking, *You did it.*

As I rode home with my neighbor, I told him I raised my hand. Man, was he excited. I was too, but I didn't realize at the time how big a moment it was for me. When I got home that night, I told my wife. We smiled at each other and gave each other a hug. I had an awesome night's sleep.

During the following months, my wife and I joined the church and were baptized. Since then we have been living in Christ on a daily basis. Am I perfect? No. Do I practice a life of praying for strength and courage, for daily guidance in getting better? Every day. I struggle daily staying in the moment, and my initial belief in Christ has slowly morphed into faith. My faith has to be exercised, and I use a variety of tools to help me grow.

Today there are bold words that represent my values. Honesty, hope, vulnerability, perseverance, love, and service are anchored with a faith that is rooted for growth. I have accepted that every day is a new day for me, and I have to surrender daily to my reliance on God and his grace. I continue to practice life. I am forever grateful.

PART 3

A PATH, NOT A PILL

No one has to stay in the slavery of addiction. A Path to Freedom from the never-ending addiction cycle of survival exists. Sadly, many will hear about the path but avoid it because entering has a cost—admitting their need, becoming vulnerable. The way out of the bondage is a beautiful irony.

- Through defeat, we find our liberation.
- Through our weakness, we can be healed.
- Through our dependence, we find our truest identity.

We face a fork in the road:

- continue to enslave ourselves in an existence that *will* destroy us but where we have the illusion of control and numbness to pain
- live fully in a world we cannot control and that *can* hurt us but where we are saved because we are

connected to relationship with ourselves, others, and God

On the one hand, living fully means we relearn how to experience the ups and downs, highs and lows, celebrations and sorrows of life. On the other hand, while the "pill" of our addiction will kill us, we don't have to feel the pain of life while it's happening, nor do we have to learn anything new that puts us at risk. We can stay, as Pink Floyd so aptly described, "Comfortably Numb." The denial of addiction begins to lift (often only temporarily) when life intervenes through painful consequences or a meaningful and wise confrontation from family and friends. These moments of defeat can often be the beginning of reprieve. Change can only begin when we become sick and tired of being sick and tired and just a little willing to look for or listen to help.

The wisdom of Scripture teaches us that the Path to Freedom is akin to the wilderness experience of the Israelites after crossing the Red Sea in search of the promised land. This path, by design, is slowly revealed to its travelers. And also as the Israelites discovered in the exodus story, it is made up of waiting as much as it is of walking. It is a slow path with no quick fixes or shortcuts. The Path to Freedom is a path of liberation that requires us to learn how to live again. We must become reacquainted with the ancient relational gifts of confession, surrender, dependence, trust, serenity, obedience, and wisdom that teach us how to live.

There is not a systemic solution to addiction. No government, church, movement, website, or medicine will solve the problem of addiction and its cycle of destruction. While those things can be platforms, tools, and launching pads for help, the solution to addiction is not a top-down institutional one but an uplifting relational one. Recovery from addiction takes place one person at a time in human relationship. The good news is that this occurs all over the world every day, one person and one relationship at a time.

Beating the odds of addiction is possible. But sadly, only a minority of people experience the solution to addiction and the freedom from it. Most people don't find freedom from addiction because they don't attempt recovery. As we reawaken to the truth of how we are created, we enter the Path to Freedom. As we walk on the path daily, we become people who have empathy, compassion, creativity, and a growing desire to genuinely serve others.

7

THE MAP TO FREEDOM

The Map to Freedom reveals where we are on the Path to Freedom. We can use it to track where we are in recovery from addiction and recovery of our hearts. The map shows us the promises that will be fulfilled as every day we admit our neediness, surrender to God, and accept the struggle of keeping heart as God leads.

The recovering addict is always grateful that God is leading, even in the struggle, because they have attempted to live without that relational leadership. They grasp Psalm 84:10, which says, "Better is one day in your courts than a thousand elsewhere," because they have already lived the "thousand" elsewhere.

The Map to Freedom is a nonlinear route to the growth we seek over a lifetime.

The first order of business is living daily toward the future we seek. The map shows how we grow one day at a time so we can grow into who we are created to be—just like trees.

The Map to Freedom

Developed by Chip Dodd

The Map to Freedom shows the process by which we move toward living the lives that allow us to leave something behind for those we love. The map reinforces the reality of having to grow over a lifetime and yet shows that there is a path and a process by which we can live powerless and empowered at the same time.

GET YOU >>> BE YOU >>> GIVE YOU

FEEL YOUR FEELINGS >>> TELL THE TRUTH >>> GIVE IT TO THE PROCESS

PASSION >>> INTIMACY >>> INTEGRITY

LIVE FULLY >>> LOVE DEEPLY >>> LEAD WELL

Day after day, year after year, they reach for the sun, drink in through their roots, bear fruit, and grow larger and more productive until they are finished. The map shows how we can do the same over a lifetime. But for now, let's look at the map as a newly recovering person coming back to life.

Get You, Be You, Give You

The first thing that happens in recovery is that we begin to return to how we are made: "get you." We let go of addiction.

Our denial and dissociation begin to fall apart. We begin to see and hope that there is a life different from what addiction has trapped us in.

The next step is to "be you." This step is the recognition of one's self as human, created a specific way, not self-made. It is the awareness that "I am a feeling creature, created for fulfillment through relational connection."

Next is "give you," which is the beginning of offering what is inside, beneath denial and dissociation, to others. In recovery, we begin to offer a new hope and new possibilities. The "give you" opens us to questions, needs, and receiving help like a child (until we grow into being able to answer others' questions, meet them in their needs, and offer help that we have received ourselves). We must remember that we never leave a child's humility behind as we become grown-ups. (The next chapter will go into greater detail on the tools we need to move along the path.)

Feel Your Feelings, Tell the Truth, Give It to the Process

We continue the process of "getting, being, and giving" by feeling our feelings, telling the truth about our hearts, and giving "it" to the process of living. The "it" we are giving to the process ends up being several things: the problem we are facing, the feelings we are having, our preconceived expectations based on our past experiences, and our distrust of God and others to come through. The process of living is owned by God, who is good, so good that he can handle all feelings and all truth telling. Our job is to submit to doing all three—feeling, telling, and giving—trusting that God knows

135

how to manage what he created. Of course, these acts will lead to more feelings and more truth telling! But the main point is that God is in control, not us. We have had enough experience with trying to control our lives, and we find that surrendering to the process is better than what we did in the past. By being willing to get ourselves, be ourselves, and give ourselves, which opens us up to feeling our feelings, telling the truth about our hearts, and giving "it" to the process, we begin to experience the gifts that willingness, truthfulness, and trust can give us.

Passion, Intimacy, and Integrity

We then move into becoming people of passion, intimacy, and integrity. We become relationally attached again and willing to be in pain about things we care about that matter more than comfort, risk aversion, or pain itself. This passion moves us deeper into the gifts of living, allowing us to be fully known and to fully know others. In this intimacy, we become relationally sturdy. As an old saying goes, "A friend will halve your sorrows and double your joys." We move into how we are created to live connected. We move into depths of intimacy, empathy with others, and compassion for others.

Because we know that we matter and that others matter too, we move toward integrity. We become trustworthy, dependable people. This change, occurring through submission to the process, makes us people who can serve others out of the gifts of creativity that we have rediscovered and are putting to use for the good (Phil. 4:8). Holding on to this newfound character is worth doing whatever is required.

Live Fully, Love Deeply, Lead Well

As we become people of passion, intimacy, and integrity, we find that we are living the lives we have always sought but never could find. We are living fully, living on life's terms, through the fulfilling experiences of others' and God's loving care, which we become capable of returning in kind. We are giving what we have because we have received in relationship what we could find nowhere else. We are able to love deeply, and in so doing, we are leading well a life that offers to others' hearts something worth keeping because it blesses them.

Those in recovery can give of themselves, having become true to who God created them to be. They are able to do this by facing and feeling their humanity, being truthful and surrendering to the process of God's ways. They then receive what they could not manufacture in their own control—passion, intimacy, and integrity—because relationship with God and others matters deeply and completely. And finally, they find that they are living fully, loving deeply, and leading well a life worth living because they are blessed, so they bless.

The paradox is that this path is not an end but a daily beginning as we grow into who we are created to be over a lifetime of daily admitting, surrendering to, and accepting how we are created.

Through this circuitous route, we become people of empathy, compassion, creativity, and service to others because we are gratefully passing forward what we have received. We never forget that we once were blind and now we see, we once were lost and now are found. We give ourselves, live the process as God leads, walk in integrity that is worth more than gold or power or drugs, and lead well a life that helps those who are blind see and those who are lost be found.

The results are not rewards; they are gifts. We did not earn them; we surrendered to them.

Those who come to the truth of how we are created and begin to live in the truth of how we are created in their daily lives become people who have grown in relationship connection and relational awareness. They have developed tolerance for vulnerability and the ability to love, having been loved. This process is the great story of the truly recovering and growing person. They know firsthand what has been done for them, where they were in addiction, what happened to bring them life again, and where they are now related to that recovery story. They wish to give of themselves, offer themselves to the process of life (God owns the process of life), live in integrity, and lead lives that leave something behind worth keeping.

Almost everyone wishes to give their gifts to others, live fully in the process of life, walk in integrity, and lead their life well. Yet these four offerings also require that we continue to admit our neediness, surrender to how we are created by God, and accept God as the leader of our lives, regardless of how "good" or "bad" our lives are going.

KATE'S STORY OF HOPE

I reached for the cold metal door of my dorm. I entered the stairwell. It was dimly lit, and I knew I was alone. I saw the trash can sitting there. I saw the boxes of cereal on the ground next to the big black rubber bin. I grabbed some Lucky Charms out of the box. I had money to buy food, but I was afraid to keep it in my room because what if I ate too much of it? I was on a starving and binging cycle. I had stopped throwing up the summer before due to a promise I had made to God when I felt like I could not stop. So now I was just binging occasionally, stealing peanut butter from my neighbor's room or taking candy from a nearby housemate.

Now, as you read this, it is very clear that I was addicted to food. I have similar stories with alcohol and cigarettes. These substances would help me mood alter in order for me not to feel my feelings. I was addicted to the rush of not eating because of the shame I felt when I ate too much, the feeling of relaxation when I would smoke a cigarette alone in my car, for example, after visiting my grandmother on her deathbed, and the elation I would feel when I would sip a glass of wine after a long day. I was always looking for a way out, a way not to feel my feelings in order for everything to be okay again. In my story, my eating disorder was a coping strategy for something much deeper: I would do anything to have the admiration and acceptance of others.

The first time I grasped the definition of codependency I was sitting on my balcony reading a book called *Codependent No More* by Melody Beattie. My therapist had told me that codependency is when you hold up a mirror and see other people's faces looking back at you and hear them saying who you are. This was me. I catered so much to what people thought about me that in order to find some relief, sometimes I would not care what people thought of me. I would rebel against the social norms in order to separate myself from the beliefs others kept about me. If I could self-sabotage, then I would not feel as hurt or as afraid. I would swing the other way too. If I wanted someone to like me, I would read their body language, research what they thought was cool, and read the situation to be what I thought they needed me to be. Before I entered recovery, I would have said that this behavior started in high school or college. However, I now see that it probably began even earlier. I had to be liked. I had to be good. I had to be enough. It was better to be what others wanted me to be than to *ever* be alone.

Rewind to thirty years ago. I have a memory of standing in my backyard. I see a blur of yellow fuzziness, green glowing leaves, and clear light. Our home was surrounded by a lush, overgrown forest. I would go outside to connect to myself or to connect to God. I was four years old, but I still remember the feeling deep inside me. I would silently ask myself if anyone would ever understand me. I remember looking up. It was as if I was searching for something or some sort of belonging. I would go back inside through the back door to where my mom and siblings were. Most of the time they were in the living room. While my mom was lying on the couch and channel 8 was playing on our gray TV tucked away in a cabinet close to the floor, I would bounce back into the room happy or jovial. I would look for something to say like maybe suggesting a snack or a show to watch. My role in my family was to be the mascot or the hero child. Sometimes I was even the scapegoat. It was my job at a young age to make sure that everyone was happy, comfortable, and having fun.

My parents did not walk up to me one day and decide to give me these job titles. I interpreted what my family needed in order for me to get my needs met. If I didn't want to be abandoned, then I would hide some of my core feelings like sadness and shame. If I wanted to be loved, then I would make someone laugh or exude sweetness. My behavior gave me the results I wanted. I used manipulation and deceit to ensure I was accepted. I was to be lively, fun loving, joyful, funny, and sociable. I think these are elements of my personality but not the entire picture. I carried many of my feelings deep in my body. I would never allow the sadness to come out unless I was overwhelmed with those feelings. I felt guilty having feelings of sadness and fear. I was afraid I was doing something wrong by not trusting God to handle my feelings. I don't think anyone knew. I barely did. My mother would talk about me being the independent child, the stubborn one, and the free spirit. I liked being tough. It helped me feel insulated, someone with strong opinions and ideas. I can see how it protected a very vulnerable part of me. Here I was four years old and addicted to the way my family saw me because I was so afraid to let my true feelings come out.

A few summers later, I remember being out on the pontoon boat with my family. We pulled up to a favorite spot that had cliffs, nature paths, and a rocky lake bottom. The water was the color of the Mediterranean Sea, while blue shimmered and reflected like glass from the sky. I was wearing a one-piece checkered bathing suit. I was upset that a rule had changed regarding jumping off the cliffs. It wasn't fair. I was told one thing in my family, then the rules would change. I wandered off alone down the rocky bank. This time when I was alone I was looking down. I was not looking for belonging or to be known. I was hurt, but I didn't feel like I could tell anyone. I looked down at the sharp rocks with the water splashing them. I thought of death. This was the first time I had thought about killing myself. *What if I just wasn't here anymore?* Okay. Stop. I had to pull myself together and go back to my family.

I was always torn between being alone and then not wanting to be alone. It was easier to get over the disappointment of the rules changing and to put on a brave, content front than it was to be alone with my feelings. I did not know how to let those feelings way back in my mind out of my mouth. I just kept swallowing my feelings and pretending I was okay.

I competed in gymnastics when I was in middle school, and I was the silly one on our team. I would rather be made fun of than be myself and be vulnerable. I enjoyed this role sometimes because I would make people laugh. Deep down I was *so* sensitive, but I was afraid to show that part of me because what if I was not accepted? I distinctly remember my coach calling me the funky chicken because I had awkward arms and legs. This hurt me, but I would just make fun of myself too because I was more liked that way.

141

Codependency can wear many different hats. It is a transactional relationship with yourself in which you trade your true heart for one that is more liked. One time on the way back from a gymnastics meet we ate at Olive Garden. I ordered the chicken alfredo. On our way home in Mom's car, I started feeling sick. I felt as if I couldn't breathe. I felt so much fear. I told my mom to pull over because I was going to be sick. I threw up chicken alfredo all over the side of the road. I still cannot eat alfredo sauce. I think my reaction was a result of anxiety about performing.

The only time I showed brokenness was when I was at church. I could cry, weep, and moan at the altar of our church. I believed God could handle my heartache. However, I never did any of these things with another human being. If I showed weakness, who would protect me? I was such a mix of strength and frailty. My mask was working really well, so well, in fact, that it didn't feel like a mask anymore. It felt like the prosthetic face that I wore to cover up my true self. I used religion to mask my feelings. I used food, I used a lack of food, I used control, and I used codependency the most to keep my feelings locked up tight. Over the years, I continued to spiral deeper and deeper into my crafted version of me. I would try to be honest with friends about feelings I was having or perhaps even share with a boyfriend about my mom being sad and my dad working a lot. But most of the time I was joyous and fun loving because that's how I was most liked. The little girl from the hill got lost inside expectations and preconceived constructs.

In my mid-teens, I had a boyfriend who was a year older than me. He had been a middle-school crush a few years earlier, and now he was my boyfriend. I couldn't believe that he really liked me. I was so good at being funny, charming, winsome, and personable. It was extremely hard for me to be vulnerable, transparent, and honest. My family lived thirty minutes from town, which was a long drive for a teenage boy late at night. Sometimes my parents would let him spend the night due to it being late. One night we stayed up way past bedtime kissing on the couch. I remember how much I loved being with him. He had such dark blue eyes and smelled of men's cologne. I felt seen and desired, the way I always hoped to feel when I was with people. I wanted to be known so bad.

The next morning I woke up foggily to my dad needing to talk to me about my mom. She had been struggling with depression most of my childhood. She would have good spells and bad spells. I walked into my parents' bathroom. My dad was sitting to the right of the bathtub on the lid of the toilet. I was not sure what was going on, but from the stare on my mom's face, I could guess. I looked at my mom as she said, "I don't want to live anymore." I told her that she had to live and that she was loved fiercely by so many people, especially my siblings and me. I remember the way the water looked. It was eerily peaceful dripping off her hair and her face. I knew I had to save her. I continued to encourage her, to convince her she was irreplaceable in our family.

I am not sure if my mother would have killed herself during that time, but I do know that I was able to take care of her in that moment. I think that memory gave me the power to think I could save people, I could talk people off the edge, I could change minds about death, and I was good at it. My mom survived that day. My dad and I have never spoken of it since. My dad called me to help him because he thought I was gifted in helping people. The more I reflect on this, the more I know that a young teenager has no place in saving a life.

My codependency continued with an eating disorder. I was losing my ability to face life the way I used to. I would lie about food and hide it under plants in my parents' sunroom. I was unable to finish a full soccer game due to the lack of calories I was consuming. I was physically and emotionally withering from an emotionally abusive relationship and from the secret I carried of my mom wanting to end her life on numerous occasions. Codependency took different forms over the next ten years. I pretended to be what other people wanted so I would be cool or liked, I drank too much to break free from the performance I was putting on, and I went too far sexually with guys in order to feel in control.

Then my rock bottom came. I had said yes to dinner to a guy friend coming to town. I didn't have a great feeling about him, but I had met him at camp years before, and what could go wrong? I knew he liked me. I thought he was cute but not really my type. I had a boyfriend at the time, but I thought dinner wouldn't be a bad idea. Plus his family was with him. Slowly over the night, he began to ask if he could spend the night at my apartment. I said okay because we both had been drinking and told him he could stay on the couch. When we got home, I went into the bathroom to put on my pajamas, and when I came out, he was in my bed wanting to watch a movie. I said okay because I felt guilty telling him no. I crawled into my bed next to him and tried to go to sleep. He kept trying to get me to roll over and kiss him. I kept saying no. He was relentless. I thought, *Well, I will just kiss him for a little while, then maybe he will stop asking me.* He didn't stop. He proceeded to go further. I had already said no three times and felt like he wasn't hearing me. He then took off my clothes. I just laid there silently crying because I didn't want to have sex with him. I didn't know what to do, so I just wanted it to be over. I was willing to do anything to get it over with. The next day I told him off, and I haven't spoken to him since. I was so worried about hurting his feelings that I did not take care of myself in the moment.

Codependency did not cause me to get date raped, but it did cause my voice to shrink. I thought I had to give people what they wanted in order for me to be okay. The last ten years I have been learning to tell the truth loudly because I do not want to be taken advantage of or allow someone to manipulate me.

These stories I share not to place blame on my parents, God, or unhealthy relationships. These are my stories. I am in recovery from saying yes to things I did not want to do. I used codependency to cope with my life. I used being what others wanted me to be as a way to feel like I belonged and was accepted, no matter the cost to my body and heart. It worked. It worked until it didn't. I did not step into my deepest recovery until several years ago. I remember sitting outside at a restaurant talking with a mentor and friend. I remember being close to who I felt I was on the inside. It took me months, probably even a year, to trust him. I started letting someone in who saw me as a gifted person and friend. I kept waiting for something I said or did to push him away. Nope. It didn't happen. The more I was myself, the more I belonged. This had never happened in a trusting relationship.

I started seeing a new therapist. She was kind, really kind, the type of genuine niceness that I needed in order to sift through some of my stories. She held the stories with care and grace as I fumbled through them, exposing parts of myself I had never shown anyone.

I don't think it was until I did EMDR therapy and the Sage Hill Spiritual Root System Training that my beliefs about myself began to change. Beliefs that were rooted really deep were that I had done something wrong, I was alone, and I was bad. I had constructed a view of myself based on my story that I was only as good as I was while performing or acting. The girl who didn't perform did not have worth. Instead, she was sad and alone. I started learning that I had inherent worth. I did not need to be afraid of being myself while showing up telling the truth. I started trusting myself again, and it felt so good.

I am still in the process of healing from my codependency struggle with wanting to believe I have to make everyone happy to be loved. This is a ginormous lie. I can show up now with no answers, no fakeness, and no false yeses. *And it is okay.* Today, instead of making other people feel comfortable, I look and listen within. I listen for God's promptings, and I try to trust that experience and believe the truth of him showing up in me. It is more of an unlearning, an undoing, and a break from my old life. I love being present, sober, and myself more than being anyone else. Telling the truth is a crucial step in recovery even though it hurts to say the truth out loud. Speaking our individual truths heals old parts of us and helps us grieve past hurts. I know that I have used my true voice in recovery. Even if my truth is rejected, it is much better to tell the truth than to create a false self.

THE FIVE TOOLS

Five tools help us successfully follow the map on the Path to Freedom. These tools deliver us from the slavery of addiction and allow us to live fully: (1) admission, (2) abstinence, (3) surrender, (4) acceptance, and (5) struggle.

Admission

The addiction cycle can be broken. The Path to Freedom begins with admission. It begins with vulnerability. Vulnerability allows a person to make a simple admission: "I have a problem. I'm not sure exactly what it is, but whatever it is, it's harmful." Admission is the first step in the journey to liberation and the most powerful tool we need to walk the Path to Freedom daily. Admission includes the following:

- acknowledging our sickness and need for help
- recognizing that our attempts to cure ourselves are harming us and that our self-protective mechanisms have become self-destructive results
- opening ourselves up to the truth that we are trapped in a cycle

Admission is a process, not an event. It requires details and storytelling, the kind of storytelling that breaks denial and moves us toward seeing, feeling, needing, talking, and slowly trusting that another way exists. Confessing that the things we use to fix our lives are now destroying us and that we can't stop is not easy. Paradoxically, we can help ourselves only when we admit that our grasp for control and power over life has made our lives unmanageable and that we are now powerless to stop doing what we do.

This admission must be done with helpful people who know the way of recovery from addiction and have walked their own Path to Freedom. (If it's not done with such people, it's only the blind leading the blind.) The helpers bear witness to the story they are hearing and testify by their own stories of recovery that it is possible to live free from addiction. The helpers remember and repeat their own experiences of admission as a living witness that real change is possible and on the horizon.

Abstinence

Another crucial tool in helping us find our way out of the addictive cycle of survival is sustained abstinence. Physically, psychologically, emotionally, and spiritually, to begin recovery from addiction toward freedom, we must stop using self-cure in order to discover new answers for our old problems. Abstinence from mood-altering substances and behaviors sobers the body and the mind and allows the heart to have a voice again. With abstinence, we can do the following:

- Physically, we can slowly create new neural pathways in our brains.[1]
- Psychologically, we can see ourselves and the world more as they are and not through the goggles of our addiction.
- Emotionally, we can begin to recognize that our addiction has kept us from developing the resiliency, skill, and maturity we need to deal with our lives.
- Spiritually, we can begin to uncover our lack of connection to God, others, and ourselves, which prevents us from having gratitude for and serenity with our lives as they are. We can also see our subtle demands that God make us happy (or our beliefs that we are responsible for God's happiness).

Coupled with admission, abstinence heals our bodies, clears our minds, and opens our hearts so we can begin to ask better questions. We slowly move from asking, "How can I feel better?" to asking, "How can I live fully?" While admission and abstinence are essential, they are never enough. Put simply, we will never say no to what harms us for long unless we find something to say yes to! The yes must involve surrendering to how we are made and who made us.

Surrender

The third tool we need to walk on the Path to Freedom is an emotional and spiritual surrender—not surrendering in hopelessness to addiction but rather surrendering to how we are created, to what we are created for, and to who created us.

The English word for surrender comes from the Old French word *surrendre*, meaning "to give up" or "to deliver over" (*sur* = "over"; *rendre* = "give back"). Surrender, the "giving back," implies that we have taken something and run away. In surrender, we return to give it back. In healing and recovering from addiction, the emotional and spiritual practice of surrender is an admission that there is something we have taken and something we need to give back.

Surrender means breaking our vows of invulnerability and giving our neediness over to God and others. We begin to practice daily laying down self-reliance and independence and letting ourselves in healthy ways be dependent on God and others who are trustworthy. In this practice, we begin to see who we are created to be and to do what we are created to do. This practice returns us to being fully present in our lives. In surrender, our defenses begin to fade, and our feeling, needing, desiring, longing, and hoping begin to return.

In surrender, we begin to give back who we truly are to the process of how life actually works in the hope that God and others will be different than we suspect. We practice accepting that no one has control over life, heartache is inevitable, and we are created to long and hope for something more than heartache—we crave wholeness. In surrender, we come to an awareness that only a power greater than our own efforts, intellect, and morality can move us toward wholeness. Wholeness means our heads and our hearts join and become capable of trusting that others may want our good.

In surrender, our dependence on God, trustworthy others, and how God made us begin to supersede independence. Presence begins to take the place of power. And the truth of how we are created begins to have its proper place, in spite of the realities of how life operates. We are created to live in dependency on God and others; we are created to become fully present as feeling, needing, desiring, longing, and hoping creatures; and we are created to live the truth of how we are created in spite of the reality that life is difficult and extremely painful.

Acceptance

The fourth tool is acceptance. Acceptance is part of the evolving work of recovery and does not occur overnight. It is not a one-time event but a daily practice that we will use the rest of our lives. Acceptance comes from turning our lives over to the care and the will of God.

The practice of acceptance moves us toward trust. Trust moves us to recognize, "I'm okay when life is not okay. God's got me, and God's lovingly present in life." Our job is to seek his will and to do his will. He is in control, not us. Our responsibility is to live in relationship as emotional and spiritual creatures who can use our brains to think and can use our voices to communicate the experiences of our hearts. And we can use our ears to listen to the thoughts and hearts of others. We live this acceptance by daily acknowledging that we are created to live fully through relationship

151

with our inner selves, which are fully known; with others; and God, who made them all. There is no end to this path, and there is much fruit to gain and much fruit to give along the way.

Struggle

To overcome addiction and live with heart, we must learn to struggle well. The deep, universal, emotional and spiritual human experience is struggle. Humans are born knowing how to struggle. We are designed for it, but our misguided pursuit of happiness, success, and accomplishment keeps us from knowing how to live.

The real fight in addiction recovery is about honestly struggling with ourselves (and with God). In the ancient Hebrew world, the word for *faithful* meant "truth, stability, or firmness." The Hebrews were born into Truth. It wasn't something they had to discover or figure out. God is I AM—the origin of all and the end of all. The Hebrews knew that God is the Truth. They were born knowing it whether they liked it or not. But they had a problem. They saw reality, and they said, "God, you're the Truth. You're the constant. You do not change. But when we look around, we see a different story. We see despair and destruction and divorce and darkness and death—plus a few pestilences and plagues. Nothing seems permanent."

Humans have always faced a conflict and a struggle. God is faithful, and life is tragic. Life is so tragic that it causes us to ask tough questions such as "Is God good?" "Is God even present?" "Does God really care?" "Am I alone?" "Am I known?" "Am I loved?"

Answering God's first question every day (*Ayeka*) is how we struggle. God is always asking us, "How are you? Where are you?" Until our last breath, God is pursuing us for relationship. Out of the breath God gave us he wants to hear from us, "Here I am. Please come find me."

CHRIS'S STORY OF HOPE

I was born in a small town to two loving, hardworking parents. My siblings and I were raised in a strict Christian home. We attended church every time the doors were open—at least it seemed that way to me! We were raised to know right from wrong and were taught the importance of a good education and the value of hard work. Neither of my parents took a drink of alcohol or smoked that I knew of.

My siblings and I were very competitive growing up, with athletics and academics being very important pursuits for us. God gifted me both athletically and academically, but I seemed to get in trouble more often than my siblings. I remember being taken into school on the first day of each school year by my mother, and she would always make sure to let the teacher know that it was okay to spank me if I got in trouble. I got my fair share of spankings at school, and they were invariably followed up by another whipping when I got home! Sports became an outlet for me, and by junior high school, I was playing football, basketball, baseball, and soccer.

I gave my life to Christ sometime during this period, probably around the age of twelve, got baptized, and became a member of the church I had always attended. I believed that Jesus loved me because that's what I had always heard growing up in church, and several of my friends had made that decision, so I felt like I should too. I don't really remember feeling any different, but I felt a little relieved to have done it. I attended a Christian all-boys summer camp for several years during this time, and I probably developed more faith during that time because of my experience with a couple of counselors who loved God and were kind and encouraging to me. However, the older I got, the more I seemed to be drawn to the things I was told I shouldn't be involved with.

For instance, I was spending the night with my grandparents one weekend, and they both smoked. I often asked (more like badgered) them to let me light their cigarettes, and during this weekend, they finally relented, and I liked it a lot. I remember how the Zippo lighter smelled when I opened it and how the cigarette smoke burned my mouth and throat when I lit that cigarette. That night I snuck down the hallway after they had fallen asleep and took two packs of cigarettes out of my grandmother's carton. When I woke up the next morning, my grandmother was sitting at the kitchen table with my overnight bag and the packs of cigarettes I had taken. She was disappointed in me for taking them and scolded me about smoking, but she never told my parents as far as I know.

Around this same time, some older kids in my neighborhood threw some pornographic magazines out the car window one summer day, and a friend and I picked them up. We took them to the woods behind my neighborhood and looked at them. I knew I shouldn't be doing that, but I hid them in an old stump and returned whenever I could sneak out. Somehow my mom found out about them, and I had to bring them home to her and she destroyed them. I felt ashamed about having them but also angry that she had found out and taken them from me! My mom always seemed to know what was going on with me, my siblings, and most of the other kids in my neighborhood.

During my freshman year of high school, I went for an overnight visit with an older brother who was in college. I drank alcohol for the first time that weekend, three or four fruit-flavored wine coolers that tasted delicious. I remember I loved the way the alcohol made me feel, and walking around that college fraternity party, I felt like I fit in and I had arrived. By the end of the night, I had gotten really drunk, and I got in a fight with one of my brother's suitemates. He never invited me back to visit, but I knew I would drink alcohol again and couldn't wait for the next time.

I excelled academically and athletically during my high school career. In my junior year, I was accepted via early admission to college. However, during my senior year, I began spending more time partying, drinking alcohol, and looking for excuses to spend the night with friends whose parents were more permissive than mine. I quit the baseball team the summer of my senior year because I wanted to go on a trip to the Bahamas and my coach wouldn't agree to it. I had never quit anything sports related or otherwise before then. I believe my addiction was already starting to make choices for me.

I went off to college, and my alcoholism/addiction flourished. I had few tools for living on my own, as I was used to being told where to go, when to go, and how to get there. I also remember thinking I was glad I didn't have to go to church anymore if I didn't want to. I remember the first week of classes stumbling home to my dorm after a night out partying and seeing students heading to their early morning classes. I thought they must be crazy to schedule classes that early! I joined a fraternity my freshman year, even though my brother strongly cautioned me against doing so my first year. He suggested I focus on my academics and the rigors of college-level work, but I didn't take his advice.

I was always able to find somewhere to go drink and someone to drink with, and I began drinking alcohol and smoking marijuana frequently. My academics began to suffer because I wasn't going to class or taking notes when I went. I would have told you then that I was loving college life, being able to drink and party like I wanted to, but it didn't take long for me to experience some serious consequences from my alcohol and drug abuse.

During my sophomore year of college, I had a particularly long run of drinking and partying to the point that I hadn't slept in several days. I had a psychotic break and was admitted to a psychiatric unit. I spent the first several days lying to all the medical professionals who were trying to help me because I was scared and ashamed to admit how much I drank alcohol and smoked weed. I also believed in my deranged mind that they were offering me medications just to see if I would take anything they offered, and so I refused all the medications for several days. I was so out of my mind that I remember watching a helicopter landing at the hospital and thinking it was the army coming to get me because the medical team, my parents, and university officials had decided that what I really needed was some discipline in my life.

One afternoon I was standing in front of a window with bars on it when I felt someone grab me from behind. It was three or four male nurses, and they forced me into my room, threw me on the bed facedown, pulled down my pants, and gave me a shot in my hip. I was out of it within seconds. My parents had signed an order for them to force meds on me so I could start getting well, and after I woke up several hours later, I agreed to take the medications the staff was giving me. I slowly got a little better, and after a month there, some high-powered psychotropic medications, and a diagnosis of major depression with psychotic features, I was released from the hospital and returned home to my parents' house. I remember sitting on the back deck, smoking cigarettes, taking pills every four to six hours, and thinking how sad it was that I might never live on my own again, drive a car, finish college, or get married. However, by the grace of God, my loving parents, prescription medications, and psychiatric therapy, I was able to get back into school.

Unfortunately, I eventually returned to hanging out in the same places, with the same people, and drinking alcohol, and after a night of drinking, I was involved in a single-car accident. I was not charged with drinking and driving because there were no witnesses to the crash and I was fortunate not to have injured myself or anyone else, but the accident didn't affect my drinking. Within a few weeks, I was hospitalized again as a direct result of my drinking and drug use. I spent about ten days in a different hospital and was discharged with some new medications and a new diagnosis: bipolar disorder with psychosis. Again, I never admitted to any nurse or doctor how much I was drinking, and I was soon back living at my parents' house. Again, by God's grace, loving parents, prescription medications, and lots of psychotherapy, I was able to get back into college and graduate with a degree in political science. It took me six years to get a four-year degree, and it was not what I had planned. (I wanted to be a pharmacist or a doctor, but my addiction had taken those choices away from me.)

I got married a couple of years after graduating from college, and I tried to control my drinking for a while because I suspected it was a problem for me. I also decided after working in sales for a couple of years that I wanted to go back to pharmacy school and work in our family's pharmacy with my dad. I became very focused on this goal and was able to gain entry into pharmacy school after making a 4.0 in all the pre-pharmacy coursework I had to take. I was mostly abstinent from alcohol and other chemicals during this period and was also able, under a doctor's care, to come off all the psych medications I had been on. I believe I was so driven to get a pharmacy degree that my addiction probably became performance.

My wife and I had our first child during my third year of pharmacy school, and I was so happy to become a father. I made the dean's list several times and graduated with honors. However, during my third year of pharmacy school, I was having some lower back pain. After hearing me complain about my back, a friend gave me a pill that he said might help. I remember very vividly the way that pill made me feel. I loved the euphoria, feeling warm, and the sense of ease and comfort I felt. The grass seemed greener, and the sky seemed bluer! I know now that it was a hydrocodone 10mg tablet, and I had unwittingly let my addiction out of the cage. I was a daily user of prescription opiate (pain) medications by my fourth year of pharmacy school and was a full-blown drug addict by the time I started practicing pharmacy.

During my fourth year of pharmacy school, I began to take pain pills every night after I got off work from my pharmacy clinical rotation. I looked forward to my nightly pills like an alcoholic craves a drink. I graduated from pharmacy school and received my doctor of pharmacy degree, passed the state and federal exams to become a licensed pharmacist, and started working at our family's pharmacy with my dad. Our second child was born about a year after I started practicing pharmacy, and we began a home renovation project. My solution to the added stress from work, a second child, and a home renovation project was to take more pain pills to relieve the gnawing feeling of fear and shame in my chest and my stomach. I somewhat knew my life was spiraling out of control due to my drug and alcohol use, but I felt so ashamed and guilty about it and was scared to ask for help. I thought I should be able to figure things out as a pharmacist and somehow get myself off the narcotics I was taking. After all, I had a doctor of pharmacy degree and knew more about chemicals and drugs than most people. However, my own best thinking at the time led me to begin taking Xanax to help manage the withdrawal symptoms I experienced when I tried to taper or stop the narcotics I was hooked on as well as the constant gnawing feeling in the pit of my stomach. I was also having trouble sleeping because the pain pills were like energy pills for me. They revved me up so much that I began taking a prescription sleeping pill to help me fall asleep.

Around this same period, Heath Ledger died of a drug overdose, and I remember reading the report on his toxicology screen. It read like a top three list of my drugs of choice, but it barely fazed me. I was drinking alcohol at social events with all the prescription medications I was taking, even though I knew this was a very dangerous, potentially fatal combination. I was rapidly approaching the bottom from my drug addiction, as it was becoming more and more difficult to function at work; hide my drug use from my spouse, coworkers, and parents; and make it through a workday. I recall one Sunday morning going to the church I had grown up in, sitting in the second-row pew with my spouse, two children, and parents, and being so high on narcotics that I thought, *God, this is why I can never quit.* I was literally vowing in church that even God couldn't help me.

I was spiritually bankrupt, keeping secrets, living a lie, and feeling so empty on the inside. I thought I had everything I believed growing up would make me happy—a wife, children, a nice house, two cars paid for, a great career making a good living—and yet I was killing myself with drugs and alcohol and couldn't stop. I knew that whatever had happened to me during my undergraduate years was happening again, and I felt totally helpless and hopeless to stop it.

One night during a New Year's Eve weekend after a particularly long day of drinking and drug use, my spouse confronted me and asked what was going on. In a moment of clarity from the chemical fog I had been in, something inside me pushed the truth out of me and I admitted that I had become addicted to prescription drugs and needed help. I recall feeling a sense of relief that my secret was finally out followed shortly by a ton of fear about what was going to happen next. I was referred to treatment by the professional monitoring program for impaired pharmacists and was given a list of eight treatment facilities to choose from. Most of the rehabs were twenty-eight-day programs, but one place was eighty-four days and specialized in treating professional men in a smaller setting, only ten patients at one time. I spoke with the clinical supervisor on the phone, and I asked him if there was any chance I could finish their program in under eighty-four days. He told me they wouldn't keep me there one day longer than I needed to be there. My ego told me I would finish treatment in record time, probably no more than six weeks. I was so sick that I was in treatment for more than twelve weeks!

I know today that God was doing for me what I couldn't do for myself by leading me to this treatment facility and putting several men in my path who would help save my life and get me on the path of recovery. My mother flew with me because I was too sick to go alone and my spouse was several months pregnant. We were supposed to arrive at the treatment facility at 10 a.m., but we stopped by a store because I didn't have a Bible and my mom wanted me to have one. She also purchased several other religious books that she knew would help me if I read them while I was in treatment.

After several days of detoxing in the local hospital, I began the inpatient treatment process, which centered on 12-step recovery, intensive individual and group therapy, and helping men recover from addiction. I knew the counselors were offering me something much better than what I was holding on to, but initially my ego and pride wouldn't let me accept their help. These men, the counselors and therapists, loved me enough to stand in my way, tell me the truth about how sick I was, and help me reach a point of surrender during the treatment process where I became willing to do whatever they suggested to stay clean and sober. I stayed in treatment for four months (I ended up staying longer than the eighty-four days) and could probably write a book about my experience during this process. The men at the treatment center showed me a new path in recovery that could keep my disease of addiction in remission. I learned that addiction isn't a matter of morals, willpower, or intellect—it is a disease I had that wasn't my (or my parents') fault, but it would kill me if I didn't get and stay in recovery.

I returned home in time to experience the birth of our child, who was so beautiful. I had a new appreciation for all the blessings in my life, and having a new baby was one of my greatest blessings as a father, especially getting to be there totally clean and sober. My discharge summary from treatment instructed me to call an 800 number every day to determine if I would have a random drug/alcohol screen that day, attend ninety 12-step recovery-based meetings in the first ninety days after treatment, get a home group at one of the meetings, find a sponsor, see a therapist as instructed, and follow all the guidelines in the five-year monitoring contract I had signed with the professional monitoring program. I wasn't allowed to return to work for six months, and this gave me a lot of time to spend with my children, go to 12-step meetings, set up a recovery network of meetings, and find friends in recovery and a sponsor to help me work the 12 steps.

I was so grateful to be back home, clean and sober, with my family and to continue growing into the man God intended me to be. The men in treatment helped me find my way to a belief that God loves me, cares about me, and wants good for me. I slowly developed a faith in God as I started seeing him work in other people's lives and eventually in my own. I returned to full-time work as a pharmacist six months after asking for help and going to treatment, and I felt so thankful going to work clean with no desire to take any type of mood-altering chemical. I had already experienced what I believe had to be a miracle: God relieving me of the relentless obsession to take pain pills and the absolute bondage that active addiction had become for me. My life was very full and busy with recovery-work meetings, therapy, 12-step work, practicing pharmacy, raising our children, and all the challenges of being married and trying to live a new way of life.

About two years into my recovery, my wife and I began to have marital problems. I was no longer interested in going to many of the social events we used to attend before I was clean and sober. Subsequently, we grew apart, and as a result of actions on both sides, we went through what was for me a very painful, scary, and sad separation and divorce. I was able to stay clean and sober during this incredibly difficult time with the help of several men in my network, including my sponsor and men I had met in treatment. One man I was in treatment with had gone through a very difficult divorce several years prior. He was able to share his experience with me during my separation and divorce to help me through them without making some of the same mistakes he had made. After our divorce was finalized, she moved out and we shared joint custody of our children. I had to do a lot of growing up during this transition in order to be a single father, work full-time, and manage a household. Eventually, I was able to see that God was doing for me what I couldn't do for myself by allowing me to go through this trial. He used it to strengthen my recovery, straighten my path, and show me that his grace and mercy were sufficient.

I have had many wonderful experiences in recovery getting to share my story with others both as a pharmacist and as a recovering addict, trying to give away to others what was so freely given to me. I finished my five-year monitoring contract with the professional monitoring program and had over one hundred negative drug and alcohol screens. I am now partner in the family business with my father, and he has been able to retire after many years of practicing pharmacy. My parents are able to travel, and they trust me to manage our family's pharmacy and take care of business. I went through a surgery around the time my monitoring contract was ending. I made sure the surgeon, anesthesiologist, and everyone else involved were aware that I am an addict in recovery from mood-altering substances. I was able to come through the surgery with a minimal amount of mild pain medication and stay clean and sober.

During this same period, I met a woman who was also recently divorced and shared custody of her only child. We fell in love with each other and have been together for several years now, raising our children together, supporting, encouraging, and loving each other. She has been very supportive of my recovery, we frequently attend meetings together, and we attend church together as we continue to grow closer to each other and to God.

I put my recovery before anything else because I have learned through this process that if I put anything in front of it, I will eventually lose. I frequently attend 12-step meetings on my lunch break, help other addicts and alcoholics, and sponsor other men. I meet with my sponsor regularly, ask God daily to help me stay clean and sober, and try to be of service to others. I love my life in recovery today, and I have learned how to live fully, love deeply, and lead well through the process of recovery. I feel my feelings, tell the truth, ask for help, don't keep secrets, suit up and show up, and trust God.

9

THE PARADIGM OF SICKNESS AND RECOVERY

Abstinence from an addictive substance or behavior is essential if recovery from addiction is to be realized. But while the physical component of addiction often seems the most difficult part to address, and though withdrawal can be terrible, by far the reasons most people do or do not recover from an addiction are emotional and spiritual.

Medically assisted treatment alone cannot do enough to help recovering addicts find the life they are made to have. Sobriety alone cannot be the goal of addiction recovery. Recovering addicts must learn to develop new skills—especially in the realm of relationship with themselves, others, and God.

Living fully happens for people who are known to themselves, others, and God from the inside out. Real freedom from addiction must include an inward growth. This growth is like the rings in a tree growing from the inside out, each year moving outward while the tree's roots grow deeper and deeper and its branches stretch for more light. Relational intimacy and connection nurture the addict in this growth and in life's most fulfilling experiences. In relationship, we experience all the good and beautiful this life has to offer, and doing so helps us to be able to weather all the pain life throws at us. In relationship, we come to know and trust love. We get to experience the lavish simplicity of things such as patience, kindness, acceptance, empathy, compassion, forgiveness, creativity, delight, safety, trust, faithfulness, and fun.

Even with all the good and beautiful that happens in life, the human experience is challenging, to say the least. Life is often painful and discouraging—especially in relationship. This is our dilemma: we are made to realize the best life has to offer in relationship, but we sometimes end up experiencing the worst. Many of the most hurtful and harmful things that we will ever go through happen in the context of relationship with others (sometimes with those we love the most and need the most love from).

Experiencing betrayal, abandonment, abuse, or neglect in relationship wounds the heart and leaves us self-protected and discouraged. We become increasingly intolerant to being vulnerable to how we are made, and we resist taking risks in relationship. However, we are still made to experience the full beauty of life that comes through intimate relationship. Therefore, we attempt to find substitutes for intimate connection without having to experience the pain that comes with vulnerability or to do the work of resiliency. Instead of vulnerability being a way to be fully present in life with others, it becomes fraught with anxious or depressing results.

The following illustration, the Paradigm of Sickness and Recovery, is a developmental perspective that shows how we gradually become lost in addiction. It also shows how we can return to full life through recovery by regrowing the capabilities of vulnerability and resiliency. The top half (the Paradigm of Sickness) shows how we develop an addiction. The bottom half (the Paradigm of Recovery) shows how we return to life from addiction.

The Paradigm of Sickness

A. *Self.* We are born with the divine capacity and potential to live fully. We each come into life a full-hearted Self. Even without intellectual acumen, physical abilities, or acquired talent, we are born with all the worth we will ever need or hope to develop. We are each born emotionally and spiritually prepared to live fully. While we will need help to nurture, steward, and shape these components throughout our lives, we are born with all the emotional and spiritual substance and quality we will ever need.

The Self is coded by creation with a specific set of behaviors that express exactly who we are created to be and what we are created to do. Three behaviors over which the human being is initially powerless occur at birth to mark us as ready to do life as we are created to do it. And these three behaviors, in more sophisticated forms as development occurs, remain with us over a lifetime.

- cry out
- reach out
- take in

The Paradigm of Sickness and Recovery

Developed by Chip Dodd

The Paradigm of Sickness and Recovery shows the long-term and developmental process that influences the "need" for addiction and other impairments as a form of protective self-cure.

When the true Self is abandoned, shame occurs as an impaired attempt of the human being to stay in relationship with significant caregivers. Staying in relationship with caregivers involves trying to become what someone will accept, which develops into the codependency self-cure to stop the shame. In codependency, the addiction to other people's approval becomes overwhelming, and attempts to find relief begin: addiction and other impairments such as anxiety disorders, depressive disorders, and personality disorders. Recovery requires going in reverse order from the impairment through codependency, shame, abandonment, and finally to the true Self. Simply put, as a person recovers, the impairment is reduced and the true Self can return.

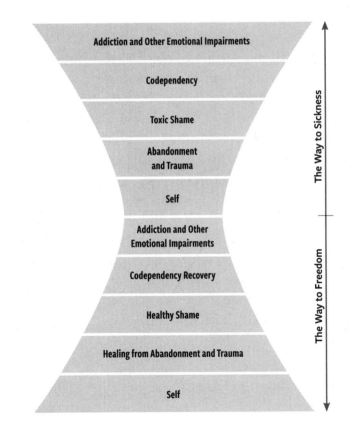

When a child is born, the child "speaks" need immediately. They cry out for connection, which will bring security through human bonding, with the inborn "knowledge" that they are created for relationship—for the sake of life's fulfillment. The child speaks the fear that acknowledges danger and need. As the child cries out, they also move toward the second behavior, which is reach out. The child reaches out for connection to a caregiver. Human touch allows the child to find a solution to the need that is inherent in the cry out. The child finds a home in the caregiver's touch. The child then, with the third behavior, takes in the food of life that not only nourishes the body but also nurtures the emotional well-being of the newborn. The child cries out for, reaches out toward, and takes in the aspects of life that relationally connect them to living well.

Though simplified, these three behaviors express the primary human needs of belonging and mattering. The needs to belong and matter are lifelong. Throughout life, both are fulfilled through our capacity to be ourselves as God created us to be: to have (1) the ability to cry out or be in need through our feelings, desires, longings, and hopes; (2) the ability to reach out toward others and God to be affirmed and confirmed in our God-bestowed worth; and (3) the ability to take in the nourishment and the nurturing that allow us to become people who can offer the world the gifts of empathy, compassion, creativity, and service to others that develop through healthy relationship.

These gifts that develop through healthy relationship with others and God allow us to become people who can live fully, love deeply, and lead well a life that blesses others with those gifts if we are allowed to develop as we are created, in relationship that affirms and confirms that we are made "right."

B. *Abandonment and Trauma.* Tragically, in many ways and in many places, instead of affirmation and confirmation of how we are created, we experience multiple forms of abandonment: rejection, abuse, betrayal, and neglect. Humans are hardwired with three fears: loud noises, being dropped, and abandonment. At a primal level, we equate all three with threats of death. The need for relational connection is so powerful that to not have it feels as if we are going to die. We need to belong and matter in relationship, or we will die. We need relationship as much as we need food, water, clothing, and shelter.

While cognition (how we think) and culture (the larger environment we grow up in beyond the family) impact us, no doubt the major influence that predicts addiction and other maladies is the relational day-to-day environment in which we are raised—that is, the family. Because as children we have no experience with the "big" world, we lose our inborn expression and trust in how we are created. We lose self-trust because we cannot help but bestow trust on our caregivers, who intentionally or unintentionally may not raise us as God created us. When a child experiences rejection from a caregiver, the child is incapable of seeing the caregiver as flawed. The child concludes that they must change and adapt in order to be loved.

C. *Toxic Shame.* As the child grows, they blame themselves for whatever is "wrong" with them. They learn to have contempt for how they are created. Therein lies the tragedy. The child becomes toxically ashamed of how they are created—to be emotionally sensitive, to be in relational need, and to take in the relational nourishment they need to fully develop as they are created to develop. The child becomes ashamed and distrusts their God-created makeup. They have contempt toward their internal experiences of feelings, needs, desire, longings, and hopes. Toxic shame is a form of contempt toward one's own makeup and toward the vulnerability and powerlessness of that makeup.

D. *Codependency*. When we as children are not accepted and affirmed for how God created us, we attempt to become someone other than who we are created to be. We manufacture a false self to protect us and help us survive. We perform for acceptance and slowly discover that no matter how much we do, it is never enough to make us feel whole or worthwhile. We inevitably lower our expectations about life, except for the mistaken belief that worth comes from performance.

We develop expressions of codependency as a form of eradicating the toxic shame that makes us experience ourselves as unlovable and worth less than others. Essentially, codependency means that our sense of belonging and mattering comes through performance. We try to earn the love and belonging we are made to receive freely.

In codependency, we are only as good as our last successful performance, whether it be a home run, an A+, a raise, or some other form of success that marks us as temporarily lovable. But we can never do enough to make ourselves whole through performing for others.

At this stage, acceptance comes from caretaking others, people pleasing, seeking approval, and achievement. Codependency demands that we look into other people's faces to see if we are okay—to see what we are worth. In codependency, we are always reading the attitudes of others (especially caregivers and authority figures) to see if we are doing what it takes to be loved.

Codependency, then, is the detachment from the true Self and an investment in creating a version of a false self that meets the stated or unstated expectations of others. The anxiety, stress, and disappointment of pursuing love become wearing, exhausting, infuriating (often hidden), and even deadly.

E. *Addiction and Other Emotional Impairments.* When the empty pursuit of codependency becomes painful enough or no longer works, the frustration and the sense of failure lead to some form of relief seeking. This is the place that is the beginning of all forms of addiction. The relief that becomes addiction takes a plethora of forms. And addiction is only one of the effects of impaired relationship that contaminate how God created us. The rejection of the self that occurs through abandonment, with its toxic shame and subsequent codependency, also leads to anxiety disorders, depressive disorders, and personality disorders, all having an intolerance for vulnerability at their core.

The Paradigm of Recovery

Once abstinence is established, the journey out of addiction follows a similar path as the journey into addiction but with glorious, life-changing effects. Since most people who fall into addiction are emotionally and psychologically underdeveloped, addicts in early recovery often do the following:

- struggle to tolerate their own emotional experience
- lack the capacity or skill to develop and maintain durable, fulfilling relationships

To develop long-term and life-giving recovery, addicts have to take responsibility to grow themselves up. This takes time. While addiction recovery is indeed one day at a time, one moment at a time, the longer a person in recovery can stay in the process and practices of recovery, the better off their life and the lives of those they love and serve will be.

A. *Self.* The road to healing starts with a commitment to return to the true Self and to living how we are designed to live. Addiction recovery begins by facing the fact that our intolerance for vulnerability and our lack of resiliency are what led us into sickness. Once we stop looking for an escape *from* life, we must also regain the presence to live *in* life. Recovering from addiction is not enough. We must also recover the life we are made to have. For most addicts, returning to Self means gradually relearning how to tolerate feelings, needs, desire, longings, and hopes. Who am I? How am I made (emotionally and spiritually)? How did I get here? How do I care for myself well? This is an essential and continuous stage in the process of recovery. Community-based recovery programs such as Celebrate Recovery and 12-step programs such as Alcoholics Anonymous offer paths that address this component of addiction recovery.

B. *Healing from Abandonment and Trauma.* Along with accepting personal responsibility and growing as a person, addicts must also specifically learn to tolerate feelings and needs. For addicts in addiction, feelings are problems to be solved. In recovery, addicts slowly begin to experience feelings as gifts and tools to help them live fully in a tragic place.

Feelings lived in relationship with one's self, others, and God lead to the gifts they are created to bring us. Experiencing this is often difficult at first. What do I do with fear?

173

How do I embrace sadness? What is the gift and what are the limits of anger? How do I handle hurt? When is loneliness good for me, and when is it not good for me? What can shame teach me? How do I respond to guilt? What is so difficult about being glad and in what ways am I grateful? Over time we begin to see the gifts that these eight core emotions have for us as we learn to trust the process and practices of recovery.[1]

- Fear helps us prepare for solutions and ask for help, and ultimately it leads to faith.
- Sadness reveals what we value and grows into acceptance.
- Anger helps us set boundaries, create order, and express passion.
- Hurt tells us when we have been injured in relationship and leads us to find the healing we need.
- Loneliness exposes our need for solitude with ourselves, companionship with others, and connection to God, and over time it develops into intimacy with all three.
- Shame reveals to us our limitations and our giftedness. It helps us recognize that we are not God. It is the root of accurate empathy and the core of humility. It also allows us to acknowledge and celebrate our gifts and to be grateful for them, as well as to acknowledge and celebrate the giftedness of others.
- Guilt alerts us to when we have done wrong or have planned to do wrong. It expresses our conscience and sets limits for us. Ultimately, it leads to the freedom

we have been looking for as we learn to make amends for the harm we have caused and may cause again.

- Gladness shows us the blessings we have and helps us express our gratitude. In time, it leads to a joy in all things and a peace that passes most others' understanding.

Just like experiencing and expressing feelings, experiencing and expressing needs are difficult in early recovery. However, since needs are the tools we have been given to help us receive healing, replenishment, and recovery, they are essential in helping us grow into who we are created to be. We must learn to get our needs met in healthy and meaningful ways. Without knowing and expressing our needs, relationship with God and others suffers.[2] Needs are vital tools for addiction recovery and living in relationship. Many people have a difficult time identifying and admitting their needs. Following is a list of some of our most important needs:

- Belonging is the need to be accepted for who we are as emotional and spiritual beings.
- Mattering is the need to be appreciated for our individual giftedness.
- Security is the need to have a "place" where we can struggle and be supported in that struggle.
- Touch is the need to be nurtured physically and emotionally.
- Grief is the need to surrender to the reality of loss; if we experience the need to grieve, we find that we are okay.

175

- Attention is the need to be recognized, tended to, cared for, and even nurtured so that we can reexperience the encouragement that comes from knowing we belong and matter.
- Sexuality is the need to feel and experience comfort and confidence in our own skin as men and women.
- Guidance is the need to be shown how to go where we have never been in life.
- Accomplishment is the need to know when we have reached diminishing returns and to stop, to celebrate the result of having given ourselves to something that matters to us, and to rest well to allow ourselves to begin anew as we move toward the "completion" of that which moves us.
- Support is the need to be continually responded to and to have our ongoing needs replenished.
- Listening is the need to have others give their hearts to us while we speak about the parts of our lives that matter most to us.
- Trust is the need to be able to depend on those who listen to us.
- Freedom is the need to be liberated from the tyranny that stops us from living fully, loving deeply, and leading well.
- Play is the need to express being fully human and not be self-conscious about it.

C. *Healthy Shame.* In the next step of the paradigm, toxic shame and family of origin come into focus. The story of our development is the primary issue. The story of our lives—the good, the bad, and the ugly—comes into focus as the human condition, even with people we love and who hunger to love us. We begin to address all forms of messages and experiences that led us away from experiencing ourselves as normal feeling human beings who were born with inherent worth. We begin to ask questions such as "When did vulnerability of being myself begin to be avoided?" "What interactions with important people in my life began to 'inform' me that being a feeling, needing, desiring, longing, and hoping creature was 'wrong'?" "How did the important people in my life teach me that feelings were not acceptable and were somehow a form of weakness?" These questions begin to open the doors to the past. They help us remember experiences denied and dissociated from and the feelings that went with those experiences. They help us address how we lost contact with the children God created us to be.

These experiences are processed with people who are empathetic, compassionate, creative, and able to serve others. They help us reduce the toxic shame and return to the healthy shame of being human. Healthy shame awakens us to the reality that we are all in need; we all make mistakes; no one has all the answers, but we all have some; no human is God; and we all need God. Healthy shame also awakens us to the need for forgiveness and the ability to offer forgiveness, because healthy shame helps us remember that we are all created of the same material. We are all human in need of relationship, as God made us. In that process of surrender we grow, we find the path to seek justice, love mercy, and walk humbly with God (Mic. 6:8).

D. *Codependency Recovery*. Finally, by addressing and healing from toxic shame, we move into healthy relationship.

We begin to face the mistaken beliefs that love and care come from performance. By acknowledging and expressing our assumed distrust and anxiety about others' rejection, we can begin to admit our inner turmoil concerning vulnerability.

In this process, distrust begins to move toward trust. The admitting of our inner feelings and attitudes is done with others who "get" what is being revealed. Risk of heart begins to be strength of fellowship instead of more rejection and judgment of the self as a failure. We find that being human is our inherent condition and that powerlessness over others is normal. (No one who is in their right mind desires to be controlled or can be in an intimate relationship with someone who covertly or overtly demands control.)

We heal from the core terror of rejection, we heal from trauma, and we move into living fully in a place that is tragic with a God who is faithful in the midst of life's tragedies. We become resilient and capable of living vulnerably.

E. *Addiction and Other Emotional Impairments.* The paradigm of recovery has turned addiction into a door we enter to move onto the path of living fully. We return to our true Self. We become people who are capable of giving ourselves away to missions greater than ourselves.

In addiction recovery it is important to recognize that the addiction never fully goes away, though it no longer controls our lives. The purpose of recovery from addiction is to move toward attaining recovery of ourselves, not so that we can have more self but so that we have a Self to give away in maximum service with empathy, compassion, and creativity. The paradigm offers a picture of a return to the path of living fully, loving deeply, and leading well a life that offers the same to others. It is a structure that points to the process every recovering addict who finds fulfillment can enter. The process isn't an end in itself. Rather, it is a path that moves us into a thousand good unknown experiences of what happens when we admit powerlessness over what stops us from living fully in relationship. It opens the door to surrendering to God so that God can grow us into who he calls us to be. It allows us to find acceptance of the way life works. We keep growing in our capacity to receive and give, and we lead others toward the same gifts of love that we have received along the way.

ANNA'S STORY OF HOPE

The first time I remember telling someone my story was when I was in my early twenties. I was deep into my first big adventure as a single Christ follower and young professional. I found myself sitting across from a stranger in a quirky, brightly colored coffee shop with the Saturday afternoon sun pouring on the table. Everything about this day was abrasively new to me. I had just moved to a new state. I was alone, attempting to navigate my way in life. I had gone to my new church and asked if there were any women who would be willing to mentor me, and this woman said yes. There she sat across from me, a total stranger, about twenty years older than me, asking me to tell her my story.

This was the first time I remember having the feeling of really and truly being seen by another human being. "Well, I've had a pretty wonderful life so far. I have the most amazing family. We are so close, and I adore my two siblings. My mom is pretty much the most incredible person I've ever met. I surrendered my life to Jesus when I was in middle school and have been following him ever since. I don't drink or party, never have, never wanted to." On and on and on the sweetness poured out of my mouth. Thankfully, this older woman had lived much more life than me, more heartache, more struggle. She looked at me with her head cocked slightly to one side and her eyes searching me and said, "Your face and neck are bright flaming red right now as you talk about your mother. What is going on inside of you?" I stared blankly at her and slowly became aware of this visceral reaction my body was having. My face and neck felt as if they were on fire. I felt so ashamed that I could not control my body's reaction.

The truth was that I was in deep pain and my family was currently in chaos. But the truth wasn't allowed to be spoken where I came from. My heart pounded, and the voice in my head said, *You must honor your family! You were put on this earth to love them, and you are so lucky to have such an incredible family. So whatever your flushed cheeks are telling you, you better tell them to shut up!* The problem was that my new mentor wasn't buying my life of sweetness and light. She saw the tension raging in me and was inviting me to venture past the family rule of "Don't speak!"

This is the story that my heart speaks, the story that has taken me more than ten years to own as my truth. As a little girl, I was pleasing—always and steadfastly sweet. Not too loud. Not too quiet. Just enough. Just enough. I look at pictures of six-year-old Anna, and I search to connect with her heart. But I can't see her. She was already gone. Away—quiet—alone—scared—frozen in time. Outwardly in my family, I worked hard to fill my role. Sweet, happy, and carefree. My job was to have the best childhood any child ever had. My grandmother used to tell me, "You're the luckiest girl in the world. No one has ever had such an amazing mother like you have." Somehow I knew that my purpose in being born into this world was to fulfill my mother's every need and desire.

Both of my parents grew up with alcoholic fathers, although neither of them would use the word *alcoholic*. My parents didn't drink much, nor could I see any outward addiction. My dad had a good, steady job and provided well for our family. My parents came to my sporting events. My house was the house where kids came and hung out. But under the surface, our household was a prisoner to my mother's need for utter and complete control. Her anxiety and rage filled the air of the house. My father's physical body was there, but I don't remember him. He was gone emotionally. He was a nonentity in the house. I was reminded on a regular basis by my mother that he was completely incompetent to do anything for himself and of his total unwillingness to care for us children. I was the youngest and the only girl, which meant that I was my mom's best friend. I was aware twenty-four hours a day of what she was feeling, what she needed, and how to say the perfect words at the perfect moment to make her okay.

I had two major comforts in life: pleasing people and food. I tried to be everything to everyone, and when the pressure of attempting that began to crush me, food would numb it all out for a moment. Be beautiful but not too beautiful, because then guys will lust after you and that will be your fault. Be athletic but not too athletic, because guys will be intimidated by you and not like you. Be strong but not too strong, because men don't like domineering women. Get good grades but not perfect grades, because then you will be too much for your friends. In high school, I would come home every day hoping that my mom was busy doing something so I could escape into dramatic soap operas, cry, and eat frosting and graham crackers . . . like an entire can of frosting until I felt sick. I remember sitting in my living room watching TV and as soon as my mom would go down the basement stairs to do laundry, I would run to the pantry and shovel as much frosting into my mouth as I possibly could without being seen.

I made my way through college and my early professional years in a continuous cycle of gaining and losing weight. I judged the success or failure of my life each month based on if I was losing or gaining weight. I believed I had a weight problem because I was lazy and undisciplined. If I could just get my act together and stick with a diet plan, then I would fit into size 10 jeans and my life would magically be perfect.

I married my husband in my later twenties. I was so magnetically attracted to him! He was independent, brilliant, and a jack-of-all-trades—it seemed there wasn't anything he could not fix! He exuded confidence and certainty. After we married, I internally breathed a huge sigh of relief that I didn't have to navigate life alone anymore. He was a man with a plan, and I signed up for his plan with all the fervor I could muster. I had no awareness of the depth of the wounds he was operating out of, and I was barely able to admit my own. I pulled out the tools I had mastered growing up, and I poured myself into the work of pleasing him. My husband was struggling with his own addiction that I could not see. All I knew was that I was desperate for him to look at me with eyes that said he delighted in me and enjoyed me. But day in and day out, all I saw was disappointment, irritation, silent rage, and disgust in his eyes. My anxiety screamed at me, *Get your rear in gear! Oh, that's right. You're lazy and just don't care enough. You're holding him back! You are the reason life isn't working*. My days began to feel like an endless list of ways I had disappointed him.

Desperate to please my husband, I pursued a new career. He thought I could do it, so I did it. I bought business suits, studied for endless exams, changed my social circles, and practiced my elevator pitches with my husband at night. Our family financial plan now hinged on me . . . it was the most weighty performance of my life. If I succeeded, I would have the love and respect of my husband forever. Fail, and I would forever be stamped with disgrace and be abandoned. The spotlight of my husband's hyper-vigilance was fixed on my every movement. I had an Excel spreadsheet with my schedule for "success" on it that my husband had made for me. Every waking moment of my life was color coded in thirty-minute intervals seven days a week. This was supposed to simplify my business and life—every thirty minutes I was supposed to check my schedule and "simply do what that thirty-minute time block said to do."

The weight of desperately trying to make myself do what that spreadsheet told me to do was daunting. I was suffocating. I felt like I was trying to run a marathon while breathing through a straw. But I wasn't even aware that I was barely breathing. I was consumed with watching my husband, being aware at every moment what he was feeling, thinking, assessing, critiquing. I truly believed that I was responsible for his feelings, his success, his failure . . . his life. The only thing that made me drag my body out of bed and get dressed every day was the thought of a Starbucks caramel macchiato with extra whip, extra drizzle, and the most sugary muffin I could find. What I really wanted was an endless plate of whipped cream and caramel sauce. What I wanted was some place away from the microscope of my husband, away from the endless recording of everything I didn't do well enough. But the recording was in my own head shouting with a megaphone. I couldn't shut it up. The best I had was a food coma. I was utterly dependent on a food high of some sort in order to show up to any part of my life.

My husband, driven by his anxiety and demand for control over life, was climbing an endless mountain of performance that extended up to the heavens. His lust fixated on some illusive point off in the distance. More money, more sex, more predictability, more . . . more . . . more. I had tethered myself to him and was trying to carry the cement bricks of his self-hatred and my own.

I couldn't climb any longer. I was nearing the end of myself, the end of my ability to make myself perform one more day. When I looked in the mirror and breathed and really looked at myself—my heart, my insides—I knew I was living a lie. There was no amount of sugar or excess food that could completely silence the truest and deepest parts of my heart. One moment, one terrifying and courageous conversation started a chain reaction of miracles. One day standing in our kitchen I fumbled to spit out some words about how miserable I was and how I felt trapped by my job. I was failing at my new career because my insides knew that it wasn't what I really wanted to do with my life. What I really longed and hoped for was to have babies and be a mom. My heart ached to be a part of creating and nurturing life. Hearing those words from me was my husband's worst nightmare playing out, and I knew it. Nothing terrified him more than the thought of having children, and this topic had been strictly forbidden in our marriage. I had never spoken of my desire. I had shut it up and tried to make it go away.

Those few words led us to a counselor's office, which led to a recommendation that my husband travel to a treatment center. One morning my alarm sounded, and I rolled over alone in my bed. In hindsight, it was a complete miracle of God that my husband was seeking help, but to me it felt like a bomb had gone off in my life. I could not make myself get out of bed. Paycheck or no paycheck, I had nothing left in me to face the day. I called a coworker who I knew was in recovery from her own alcoholism. I told her I wasn't coming to work and that I couldn't get out of bed. She said, "Okay, I get it. You're in crisis. Don't come to work, but you're going to get out of bed, take a shower, and find an Al-Anon meeting. Text me which meeting you're going to. Text me when you leave and when you get home."

I have no idea why I did what she told me to do that day. I don't remember one word spoken at that meeting, but I remember feeling like I could breathe for the first time in a long time. I didn't say a word. I sat and let tears quietly flow from my eyes. I did not know before then that there was a place for me to go for *me*. Not to help my husband . . . not to help my mother . . . not to perform for anyone else in the whole world. Just for me. There was a chair for me in a place that was safe. I could sit and feel and say (or not say) whatever I needed or wanted to say and be met with kindness and zero demands. I had never experienced that in my life—the safety of not feeling used by another human being.

My husband was in treatment, and I had three months to breathe my own air and remember that I was a separate human being from him and responsible for my own life. I started to look in the mirror figuratively and literally. I walked into my first meeting that focused specifically on my food addiction and said out loud, "I am powerless over food, and my life is unmanageable." I asked the first person who smiled and introduced herself to me that day to be my sponsor.

I started calling my sponsor, identified my "alcoholic foods," started abstaining from them, and started working the 12 steps of Alcoholics Anonymous. Today I chuckle at writing that sentence. The words on the page don't convey the utter miracle of me going one day, let alone a week, a month, and now years, without the drug of sugar that enslaved me. It was a terrifying process to put down the only tools I had known in life. I felt like I was standing on the edge of a cliff, and not using my "drugs" was like having to step off the cliff into thin air. My sponsor and others in recovery told me there would be solid ground under me once I stepped off, but I was pretty sure I was just going to die. Miraculously and begrudgingly, I stepped off! God did in fact meet me there and put solid ground under me where I couldn't see any.

The gift of sobriety is a step, and then there is so much more to come! Action, movement, baby steps, more, more, more . . . there is always more to grow into! I have to keep moving toward God and toward others in relationship to stay in the rich life I am privileged to have today. I have received so many miracles on this journey, and I can truly tell you that I have never regretted what pursuing recovery has cost me in terms of time, money, energy, etc. It doesn't even measure on the scale in comparison to the physical, emotional, and spiritual freedom I can live in today. In closing, I would like to share with you a letter I recently wrote to my precious son.

To my beautiful, stouthearted son,

My heart . . . I want you to see and know my heart as much as I long to see and know and be with you. Our Lord, Jesus, hand-formed me and you in glorious mystery, complexity, and beauty! I am your mama, and it is not lost on me what a deep and profound privilege this is. Today I am taking stock of the fact that I could have missed you . . . your existence is truly an amazing miracle. You see, when I was growing up, I hid myself deep, deep away in silent frozen places internally because I wasn't safe. Instead of exploring how to be Anna, I learned how to be what I perceived the people closest to me wanted me to be. Accusatory, shaming, and mean voices took up residence in my head and fed me lies day in and day out. I believed those lies, and I worked so hard to try to accomplish what they demanded of me. I believed a great, terrible, and deadly lie that I would be utterly abandoned and alone if I did not please them. Even the sweet voices of Jesus and your daddy got perverted and twisted. The lies filtered every word I heard and kept me isolated from the light of love. I could not receive or give real intimacy and love. I was alone in a prison built by lies in my mind.

I want you to know that this tragedy happens for so many people on this earth. You will encounter so many people who are trapped in this same prison. Many of them, like me, find something to numb the voices and the terrible pain of isolation. I chose food and performing well, but it matters little what the vehicle is. They all lead to addiction and more slavery. Know that inside every human there is a beautiful, whole, and true person created by God just like you and me. Son, I pray and hope desperately that you will never have to experience this lostness I'm speaking of, but if it is part of your journey, please know that there is always a way back home . . . to your true place. Both your daddy and I have taken this journey back home. We recovered our precious hearts so that today we can be as whole and as present as possible with you!

I have fought for the last seven and a half years to clear away the wreckage of the voices that lived in my head so that I could uncover and be Anna. I fight to create safety so that my heart can step out from the dark corners into the light of day and speak and live free. "It is for freedom that Christ has set us free." Freedom has very little to do with money, circumstances, or position in life. Freedom is a state of being. Today I am free to be me. Today I am free to see my own beauty and even to enjoy being uniquely Anna in all my gifts, strengths, weaknesses, and even failures. Today I work to believe and live from the truth that the richest gift I can give you, your daddy, and the rest of the world is quite literally my authentic presence.

Today you are two-and-a-half years old, and I pray that on whatever day you read this when you are much older that you can wholeheartedly nod your head and say, "Yes, my mama is still living in this process of recovery today!" I committed first to God and myself and then to your daddy and you that I will stay in this process of recovery . . . to live from a place of honesty, integrity, consistency, and vulnerability, surrendered to God.

But oh, the struggle of life is so real! This commitment has to be driven so deep in my soul because life can be tragic beyond comprehension! This is the part of life I know I cannot protect you from, so I ask the Lord Jesus to help me be so present with you in it! Life is tragic, and God is faithful.

There is no way to live life so that you avoid tragedy . . . even in recovery. There is no way through except by honest struggle. I remember a dark place of struggle for me three-and-a-half years into recovery. I had fought so hard for so many years to find the courage to give voice and space to my intense desire to create life with your daddy. I uncovered this passionate flame in my heart and worked to protect it and give it a voice and space. As long as I can remember, I have longed to be your mama, even though I did not know you yet! The biggest miracle happened, and I became pregnant with your big sister! But she never breathed the air of this world. She passed and went to heaven to be with Jesus. This was such a dark time for me because it felt cruel beyond what I could bear. The whole world felt unsafe and dark. Even God felt unsafe. I am just a limited human, and I had no framework for losing my sweet baby with no explanation . . . no public acknowledgment of her life . . . no opportunity to see her face and know her heart. All I could do was beg God for the willingness to get out of bed each day and show up in some way to the daily routines of my recovery. Drag myself to a meeting, make a phone call, talk to someone who loves me, breathe, and try to give myself permission to struggle.

It was Christmastime, and I had bought a few crimson lilies and put them in a vase on the dining table. I felt lost at sea, tossed around by the waves of grief, anger, and loneliness. I felt aimless and hollow. One late morning I walked out of the bedroom, and the crisp winter morning light hit the dining table. There was this giant blood red lily that had burst wide open overnight. It was so vibrant . . . so alarmingly beautiful . . . so naked in how vulnerably it spread its petals out as wide and as far as it could! It spoke to me. "Look at me! Look at how beautiful I am! Look at how exquisitely I am made!" This lily had no concern of how long it would be alive. It was a cut flower and would not last more than a week. All I could hear and see was that right now today it was beautiful and full of life and was going to use every ounce of energy to take up space and display the inherent beauty it possessed unabashedly.

The image of this lily reaching out for life ministered to my soul in profound ways that I can't explain. It doesn't make sense to me, but beauty is healing if I have eyes to see it and an open heart to receive it. This image took root in my soul and has come to represent who I want to be in life. I want to be the beautiful person my Creator made me to be. I want to take up space and vulnerably display my beauty, to share with others today regardless of the celebration, tragedy, or mundane parts of life happening at the moment. This moment helped me keep moving so that I could keep living and receive the gift of being your mama today. No matter what, there is always more good ahead, more richness, more beauty. Keep heart, my love!

Love, your mama

10

KEEPING HEART

The Scriptures are full of stories of what it means to struggle well and successfully. From Genesis 3 to chapter 22 of the book of Revelation, the Bible records stories, parables, and proverbs about everyday people who are willing to openheartedly tell the truth about their experience and struggle to be in relationship with God, others, and themselves. One clear example of a person moving from the cycle of survival onto the Path to Freedom is Jacob.

In Genesis, we read the dramatic story of Jacob (whose name means "usurper"[1]), who is fooling himself and others and thinks he can fool God. He's always cutting a deal. He's always looking for the easy way. He's always trying to control the outcomes. He's always trying to figure out how to come out on top.

For Jacob, who in redemption becomes the father of the people of Israel, it is trouble right from the start. As the story goes, Jacob, with his mother's encouragement, manages to trick his father into giving him his older brother's birthright by means of an elaborate deception. His brother, Esau, becomes so furious that he vows to kill Jacob. At his mother's urging, Jacob flees his brother's wrath and takes refuge with relatives (his mother's brother, Laban). After years of living with his uncle, Jacob has amassed a large fortune. But even with all his wealth and comfort, he still longs to go home.

This is where the story turns. Jacob sets out with his wives and children (and wealth) to return home and seek reconciliation with his brother, Esau. Still trying to cut a deal to appease Esau's wrath, Jacob prays to God and gives his brother gifts. As he is getting closer to home, he is growing more anxious—sure that Esau is going to kill him. The night before he meets his brother he sends his wives, children, and belongings across the river, and he is alone.

So Jacob was left alone, and a man wrestled with him till daybreak. When the man saw that he could not overpower him, he touched the socket of Jacob's hip so that his hip was wrenched as he wrestled with the man. Then the man said, "Let me go, for it is daybreak."

But Jacob replied, "I will not let you go unless you bless me."

The man asked him, "What is your name?"

"Jacob," he answered.

Then the man said, "Your name will no longer be Jacob, but Israel, because you have struggled with God and with humans and have overcome."

Jacob said, "Please tell me your name."

But he replied, "Why do you ask my name?" Then he blessed him there.

So Jacob called the place Peniel, saying, "It is because I saw God face to face, and yet my life was spared."

The sun rose above him as he passed Peniel, and he was limping because of his hip. (Gen. 32:24–31)

The next day Jacob meets Esau and is welcomed by him.

Of the many amazing things about this story, one important point is that it is through struggle that Jacob receives his blessing. He receives a blessing for fighting. He receives a blessing for showing up emotionally and spiritually and for wrestling with the being of God. He receives a blessing for trying to keep his false identity, trying to have his way, trying to have control, trying to hold on and still have a life. He ends up losing his ego and gaining himself. In spite of Jacob's outward actions and self-focused attitudes, he encounters God. It is a moment of desperation for Jacob, and God meets him there—maybe not exactly as Jacob expected, but Jacob gets what he really needs, not what he thinks he needs.

His hip is injured, and his name is changed. He is broken of his perfectionism, self-centeredness, and control. He moves from being a survivor to getting on the path of being a full-hearted person. God blesses him with a new name, Israel, which means to struggle with God and live—to struggle with God and in doing so find full life. From then on, with every step he takes, he walks with a limp that reminds him of being human.

This is not a simple story and not at all what we would expect from faith perspectives rooted in merit, morality, and work ethic. It is a story of grace and unmerited favor. Jacob gets the blessing because of God, not because of himself. Blessings in an Old Testament sense aren't always warm and fuzzy. It's more of a modern notion that blessings make life more comfortable and easy. In fact, blessings are God's gifts to us that bring us into alignment with the kingdom. The expulsion from the garden is a blessing. The exodus is a blessing. The dark night of the soul is a blessing—though it never makes us more comfortable.

This Jacob story is a dark night of the soul story—a theme central to the Jewish and Christian identity. It teaches us that it is in our genuine struggle with God about life that our true identity in him is formed and revealed. Even if our motivation is not always pure, God joins us in the struggle. Even when we are struggling for our comfort (as in addiction), he is struggling with us for our liberation in him, and our character is shaped in the process. Jesus is the ultimate picture of God meeting us where we are before we are ready to meet God. God continues to make himself low and to meet us on our terms. We don't have to ascend to being better or good enough for God to meet us and participate in our lives and healing.

The name Israel is an offer for all of us. Only in our ability to struggle do we reconcile the conflict between love and tragedy, have fulfilling relationship with others, and find freedom from addiction. Like Jacob, we need to struggle with ourselves and God, walk in faith, remember our neediness (the limp), and receive our blessing. Struggling well is a requirement we face daily in order to experience freedom from addiction and recovery of heart.

WIPs

Moving into genuine freedom from addiction and genuine recovery of heart requires facing our condition: we are made to desire more than life can deliver. Our dreams will always exceed our efforts to fulfill them. Therefore, struggling well to receive the benefits of the blessing of being human begins with facing the fact that from the beginning of our lives until the end of our lives, we are works in progress (WIPs). Being a WIP means that we are going to mess up, miss something, forget something, ignore something, turn against something, bump into something, walk over something, or not know something as we pursue dreaming and hoping, living and loving. No matter what we do, we will always be like giraffes running on ice—clumsy.

In addiction, we see our humanity as our problem. In recovery from addiction, we see even our clumsiness as a blessing—we are free to be dependent and we are free to make mistakes. Our job is to grow into relationship with ourselves, others, and God. Recovering from addiction is a process of relearning to trust God, to trust others so we can find our fulfillment in relationship, and to trust how God made us as dependent creatures.

God created us to be human—which means we are feeling, needing, desiring, longing, and hoping creatures.

To stay on the Path to Freedom, we relearn the language of the heart. We relearn to identify what we feel and need. We learn how to explore the experiences of what our feelings are connected to (both present and past). We find trustworthy people who know how to handle our hearts and our stories. Identifying, exploring, and expressing our hearts keep us in relationship and expose our continual need for God and others. This practice of appropriate vulnerability is the essential element that allows us to live life fully and stay in freedom from addiction. Everyone needs recovery of heart. In our lust for control and comfort, we are all addicts in some form or fashion. Attempting to live without recovery of heart requires that we remain detached from God, others, and ourselves— detached from love.

If we miss love, we miss life completely. Love is worth the pain of attachment in a world that is imperfect, even tragic. No one overcomes life; it takes a lifetime to learn how to live. We need to work at being WIPs, because that is our true condition. Anyone who demands more is also demanding to find some way around life, which always leads to addiction. Denying what it means to be human leads to the hubris of trying to be God instead of being a human in need of God.

Being a WIP isn't the end of things as much as it is the beginning of growing into who we are created to be. We remember mercy because we know we need it. We have compassion because we are all in the same condition. We have new courage because we care more than ever before. We have a desire to serve others as we have been served. Our lives, in recovery, become a reflection of the Beatitudes from the Sermon on the Mount. We see our blessings and become blessings to others through our defeat, grief, meekness, and hunger and thirst for more. Being a WIP makes a lot more room for God's presence in our lives because we have faced the fact that we are not God. Instead, we are marvelously human—created by God and in need of the One who created us.

Daily Practices and Disciplines of WIPs

As works in progress, we practice but never perfect some basic daily actions. These actions teach us how to live and allow us to stay on the Path to Freedom. When we first begin down the Path to Freedom, these practices can seem unnatural and forced. As addicts, we will even try to use them as ways to control outcomes instead of as ways to help us live the best lives we can have on life's terms.

There are many great books, podcasts, and other resources related to each of these practices. The practices include the following:

- prayer
- spiritual reading
- journaling
- vulnerable, intimate relational connections with mentors (sponsors) and peers, and recovery meetings with recovering people
- rigorous honesty
- maintaining a clean slate of forgiveness
- caring for one's own emotional, spiritual, and physical health
- serving others
- gratitude

As we follow these practices, the great paradox of Matthew 18:2–5 becomes a reality.

He [Jesus] called a little child to him, and placed the child among them. And he said: "Truly I tell you, unless you change and become like little children, you will never enter the kingdom of heaven. Therefore, whoever takes the lowly position of this child is the greatest in the kingdom of heaven. And whoever welcomes one such child in my name welcomes me.

Jesus spoke these words as a response to his disciples' asking him, "Who, then, is the greatest in the kingdom of heaven?" (v. 1). In his response, Jesus showed them that the one who is dependent, the one who is the most vulnerable, the one who is the most truthful about their human condition will grow into someone who lives fully, loves deeply, and leads well. People like this live lives that are blessings to others now and in the future. The greatest human fulfillment is to become a person of maximum service. People who are in recovery from addiction and recovery of heart live a blessing that others don't have and develop a wisdom that others can't have. Because of their limp, they travel a narrow Path to Freedom that gradually becomes a meadow. They live on the edge of a vista in sight of the kingdom of heaven. These people become sure of what they hope for and certain of what they do not see. Their daily lives are ordered around a big life of love, passion, and eternity. Their lives become greater than themselves without their ever seeking greatness.

A famous expression of this process was written by Reinhold Niebuhr. When practiced daily, it becomes a reminder of where we were, what happened, and where we are now. It encourages us to live life on life's terms in relationship with a God who loves us.

The Serenity Prayer

> God grant me the serenity
> To accept the things I cannot change;
> Courage to change the things I can;
> And wisdom to know the difference.
>
> Living one day at a time;
> Enjoying one moment at a time;

Accepting hardships as the pathway to peace;
Taking, as He did, this sinful world
As it is, not as I would have it;
Trusting that He will make all things right
If I surrender to His Will;
So that I may be reasonably happy in this life
And supremely happy with Him
Forever and ever in the next.
Amen.

Reinhold Niebuhr (1892–1971)

NOTES

Introduction

1. REM, "Losing My Religion," *Out of Time*, Universal Music Publishing Group, 1991.

Part 1 The Age of Addiction

1. Andrea Tone, *The Age of Anxiety: A History of America's Turbulent Affair with Tranquilizers* (New York: Basic Books, 2012), 153.

2. Robert Bennett, "Aldous Huxley Foresaw America's Pill-Popping Addiction with Eerie Accuracy: We're Now Living in the *Brave New World*, Literary Hub, March 21, 2019, https://lithub.com/aldous-huxley-foresaw-americas-pill-popping-addiction-with-eerie-accuracy/.

Chapter 2 The Pandemic

1. "2018 NSDUH Annual National Report," SAMHSA, August 20, 2019, samhsa.gov/data/report/2018-nsduh-annual-national-report.

2. Krishnadev Calamur, "An 'Overprescription of Opioids' That Led to a Crisis: The Director of the National Institute on Drug Abuse Pointed to Economic Factors as a Cause of the Epidemic," *Atlantic*, June 23, 2018, https://www.theatlantic.com/health/archive/2018/06/opioid-epidemic/563576/.

3. Calamur, "An 'Overprescription of Opioids.'"

4. CDC/NCHS, "National Vital Statistics System, Mortality," CDC WONDER, 2018, https://wonder.cdc.gov.

5. https://www.pornhub.com/insights/2018-year-in-review#us.

6. Josh McDowell Ministry, "The Porn Phenomenon," Barna Research Group, 2016.

7. Josh McDowell Ministry, "The Porn Phenomenon."

8. "Statistics of Gambling Addiction 2016," North American Foundation for Gambling Addiction Help, accessed February 19, 2020, http://nafgah.org/statistics-gambling-addiction-2016/.

9. "Eating Disorder Statistics," SCDMH, accessed February 10, 2020, http://www.state.sc.us/dmh/anorexia/statistics.htm.

Chapter 3 The Emotional and Relational Costs of Addiction

1. Laura Lander, Janie Howsare, and Marilyn Byrne, "The Impact of Substance Use Disorders on Families and Children: From Theory to Practice," *Social Work in Public Health* 28, no. 3–4 (May 2013): 194–205.

2. A. Berkowitz and H. W. Perkins, "Personality Characteristics of Children of Alcoholics," *Journal of Consulting and Clinical Psychology* 56, no. 2 (1988): 206–9.

Chapter 4 What Is Addiction?

1. Marc Lewis, *The Biology of Desire: Why Addiction Is Not a Disease* (New York: PublicAffairs, 2015), 42.

Chapter 8 The Five Tools

1. In terms of physical addiction, this can be so difficult that in some cases medical assistance is required.

Chapter 9 The Paradigm of Sickness and Recovery

1. For more in-depth exploration of the eight feelings, see Chip Dodd, *The Voice of the Heart: A Call to Full Living* (Murfreesboro, TN: Sage Hill Resources, 2015).

2. For more information about needs, see Chip Dodd, *The Needs of the Heart* (Murfreesboro, TN: Sage Hill Resources, 2017).

Chapter 10 Keeping Heart

1. Gen. 25:26. Jacob's name (*Yaakov* in Hebrew) literally means "grabber." In the Genesis narrative, Jacob is so called because during birth he grabbed Esau's heel. Esau says of Jacob, "Isn't he rightly named Jacob? This is the second time he has taken advantage of me. He took my birthright, and now he's taken my blessing" (Gen. 27:36). The prophet Hosea indicts Jacob for "supplanting" his brother (*akav*, a pun on the name *Yaakov*).

Chip Dodd, PhD, LPC-MHSP, is a consultant, mentor, and counselor who has worked in the field of recovery from addiction for over thirty years. He is the founder of the Center for Professional Excellence, a treatment center for professionals, and Sage Hill, a social impact organization. He is the bestselling author of several books, including *The Voice of the Heart*, *The Perfect Loss*, and *Parenting with Heart*. He and his wife have two grown sons and live in Murfreesboro, Tennessee.

Stephen James, MA, LPC-MHSP, NCC, is the founder and executive director of Sage Hill Counseling in Nashville and the creator and CEO of The Leadership Lab, which helps entrepreneurs, executives, and professionals improve not only their leadership but their family lives as well. He is the bestselling author of six books, including *Parenting with Heart*. He and his wife, Heather, live in Nashville, Tennessee, and have four children.

Connect with
Chip Dodd

Visit Chip online at **ChipDodd.com**
for podcasts, videos, a blog, and more!

Chip Dodd, PhD, is the founder of Sage Hill:
A Social Impact Organization and the Center
for Professional Excellence.

v ChipDodd   **f** ChipDoddPhD   **y** ChipDodd

Connect with
Stephen James

Founder and Executive Director
of Sage Hill Counseling

Creator and CEO of The Leadership Lab

SageHill.co | The LeadershipLab.co

in Stephen James, LPC-MHSP, NCC

⊙ SageHillCounseling

⊙ TheLeadershipLab.co